SIMPLY GOOD

Peter Sidwell's
family
food

80 fabulous recipes for
every day of the week

Dedication

I would like to dedicate this book to my grandparents Geoff, Sadie, Brenda and Jim, and to all grandparents who do such an amazing job supporting their families

Also by Peter Sidwell

Simply Good Taste
Simply Good Bread
Simply Good Pasta

Recipe notes

All recipes serve 4 unless otherwise stated.

All teaspoons and tablespoons are level.

Both metric and imperial measurements have been given in all recipes. Use one set of measurements only and not a mixture of both.

All cooking times are approximate and will vary in accordance with the type of cooker hob, conventional or fan oven used.

Please be advised this book includes recipes where nuts have been used.

Eggs should be medium unless otherwise stated.

Photograph on page 4: Beef in beer, see recipe and tip on page 80.

First published in Great Britain in 2012 by Simon & Schuster UK Ltd
A CBS COMPANY

Text copyright © Peter Sidwell Media Ltd, 2012. All rights reserved.

www.simplygoodtaste.co.uk

Photographs copyright © Richard Faulks, 2012. All rights reserved.

1 3 5 7 9 10 8 6 4 2

SIMON & SCHUSTER
ILLUSTRATED BOOKS
Simon & Schuster UK Ltd
222 Gray's Inn Road
London
WC1X 8HB

www.simonandschuster.co.uk

Simon & Schuster Australia, Sydney
Simon & Schuster India, New Delhi

Editorial director: Francine Lawrence
Project editor: Sharon Amos
Designer: Geoff Fennell
Photography: Richard Faulks
Production manager: Katherine Thornton
Commercial director: Ami Richards

A CIP catalogue record for this book is available from the British Library

ISBN 978-0-85720-314-4

Printed and bound in China
Colour reproduction by Dot Gradations Ltd, UK

SIMPLY GOOD

Peter Sidwell's
family food

**80 fabulous recipes for
every day of the week**

SIMON &
SCHUSTER
ILLUSTRATED

London · New York · Sydney · Toronto · New Delhi

A CBS COMPANY

Contents

Family food

This book has been in the making for the past four and a half years, since I became a dad – the best job in the world. I started creating it the very day I began cooking for my family. It's a very organic and honest book – I've lived and breathed it every day and it's been a great opportunity for me to create a truly useful family cookbook.

I have written the recipes to reflect everyday events in family life and I hope you will be able to dip into this book at any time and find something perfect for your family. Although I'm a professional chef with my own cookery school, please remember I don't write my cookbooks to dictate to you what and when you should cook. What I'm hoping is that these recipes will give you the confidence to run with them. So if you don't have a certain ingredient in the cupboard to make a dish, don't give up and reach for a ready-meal from the freezer – look for an alternative instead.

Make these recipes your own and enjoy them!

Cooking for the family

I love nothing more than cooking for my family – unless it's cooking for friends too. And my aim is to create the right type of dish for the right environment. I always try to plan our family meals. I usually sit down with my wife on a Sunday evening and look at what's happening over the coming week, and plan accordingly. If there's a busy day coming up then I'll cook something fresh, fast and simple that I know we will all enjoy – that's where the I'm Starving! chapter comes into its own. The last thing you want to be doing is a slow-cooked stew or roast when the kids have got a dance class or football practice that evening, so choose one of these quick tasty dishes.

If you've got friends coming for Sunday lunch then it's time to look in the Weekends chapter for a scrumptious roast. Or delve into Easy Entertaining for a little something beyond the usual dinner-party food that always seems to get rolled out wherever you go.

If the sun is out and you're planning a picnic, turn to the Days Out chapter, which is full of tasty treats that you can cook outside, as well as recipes to make at home when you've been fruit picking or fishing.

Now, I live in the Lake District, one of the wettest areas in the UK, so a chapter full of baking ideas for the kids is a must when they're climbing the walls stuck indoors on a rainy day. If I suggest a baking session my daughter Poppy has her very own cooking apron on quicker than I can get the pots and pans out. Kids love cooking and are more likely to try something new if they have made it themselves and you'll find lots of recipes to get them started in my Rainy Days chapter.

Start with shopping

For me the most important part of cooking is to go for good quality when shopping. If you buy good-quality ingredients, half your work is done – they need less doing to them. When cooking with good-quality ingredients, less is definitely more.

Then I always try to let seasonal food dictate what I cook. If a food is in season, it is likely to be better quality and a little cheaper. There is nothing more ridiculous than buying strawberries in January for £4 a punnet. If you need fresh strawberries for a recipe in January, you need to look for a different recipe. Check my seasonal food list on page 10 for some help.

More than just putting food on the table

Good cooking should be a great reason for the family to gather around the table and enjoy not just the food but each other's company and hear about each other's day. Food is the glue for a family: it gives real purpose to the day and gives you something to look forward to. I like nothing more than sitting down and hearing about what my wife and children have done today, be it spelling a word at school or how many times we've had to read *The Gruffalo* – it matters!

Introducing kids to food

Since becoming a father I've realised how important it is to cement a good relationship with food for children. I have seen so many children who are terrified of trying different foods. It's a battle of wits and often, just when you think you have cracked it, it turns out you haven't.

As some of you will know already, my cooking is bold, brave and full of flavour, and I've found that when kids are young they actually enjoy strong tastes. Don't be afraid to let them try an olive or tuck into a cube of feta; the more foods they are exposed to, the more they will become familiar with different tastes and textures. This can only help them develop a good relationship with food for the future – that's my theory anyway.

Please don't think I do this all on my own, as my wife Emma plays a big part. Together we try to involve our family in all aspects of food and cooking. Poppy, our four-year-old, is good at finding different ingredients in the supermarket. We always explain to her what the item is for and when we are eating it. I think this is an important part of the process: it's like joining up the dots until we get to the end – sitting down and eating.

Now, everything I've talked about here certainly does not amount to sure-fire, hard and fast rules: this is a working project and we as a family still have a long way to go until my wife and I pack the kids off to university as five-a-day-eating adults. I will keep you posted – but I do feel we are doing the right thing.

Make things easy for yourself

Like most working parents, I don't want to be a slave to the kitchen. When I get home after work, time with my children is important – rolling around the floor being jumped on or playing hide and seek is more important. A few gadgets in the kitchen can really help save time.

Slow cookers have been a revelation for me. I am a complete convert – I love them. You can't fail to make a great stew with some good-quality hand-diced shin of beef, a good bottle of local beer, a stock cube and a few chopped root veggies. Stick them on to slow cook all day and when you get home from work you'll have a wonderful dish that will truly taste fantastic.

I also have a bread maker. Now don't get me wrong, I love nothing more than chucking some bread dough about in the kitchen and rustling up a golden crusty loaf or a simple tomato, mozzarella and basil pizza. But my bread maker is great for making a basic loaf or taking the hard work and elbow grease out of making a good dough.

Keep on tasting

When you are cooking, please, please taste your food as you go along. It is one of the most important pieces of advice I can give you. Dishes change in flavour during the cooking process, so it is crucial that you taste and season with some of the following: salt, pepper, herbs, lemon juice and vinegars. These are all ingredients that can raise the profile of your cooking and professional chefs use them to balance flavours, textures and tastes.

Happy cooking!

Seasonal food

I believe in eating food in season – not only does it taste better, it's often cheaper too, as it hasn't been grown in a greenhouse then flown halfway round the world. Here's my guide to what's seasonally available in greengrocers, supermarkets, market stalls and farm shops.

Spring

Asparagus
Broad beans
Brown crabs
Cabbage
Lovage
Mussels
Purple sprouting broccoli
Sea bass
Spinach
Spring lamb
Spring onions
Watercress
Wild garlic

Summer

Apricots
Aubergines
Beetroot
Cauliflowers
Cherries
Cobnuts
Cornish sardines
Courgettes and their flowers
Cucumbers
Damsons
Elderflowers
Fennel
Fresh (wet) garlic
Fresh (wet) walnuts
Globe artichokes
Green beans
Greengages
Haddock
Jersey Royal new potatoes

Lamb
Langoustines
Mackerel
New season's carrots
Peas
Peppers
Pigeon
Salad leaves
Samphire
Soft fruit, including strawberries, raspberries, blueberries, gooseberries, loganberries, blackberries (late summer), blackcurrants, redcurrants, whitecurrants
Spinach
Tomatoes
Whiting
Wild salmon
Wild trout

Autumn

Apples (British varieties)
Celeriac
Damsons
Elderberries
Figs
Kale
Mackerel
Maincrop potatoes
Marrows
Mushrooms
Pears
Pheasant and other game birds
Plums

Pumpkins and squash
Quinces
Rabbit
Red mullet
Sea bass
Shallots
Sloes
Sweetcorn
Swiss chard
Wild mushrooms
Wild sea bass

Winter

Brassicas, including cauliflowers, cabbage, red cabbage, Brussels sprouts, cavolo nero (Italian cabbage)
Celery
Chestnuts
Goose
Jerusalem artichokes
Leeks
Maincrop potatoes
Partridge
Rhubarb (forced)
Root vegetables, such as carrots, swedes, turnips, parsnips, celeriac
Sea bream
Venison

I'm starving!

We've all been there: the kids are hungry, you're hungry and all you want to do is get food on the table – fast. This chapter is full of recipes you can knock up in a flash. Although speed is of the essence, that doesn't mean you have to compromise on taste and quality. Some of my greatest dishes have come from raiding the cupboards and fridge when I'm up against the clock.

Tomato and preserved lemon soup

I love tomato soup, and here I've seasoned it in classic Moroccan style, which gives the soup an amazing depth of flavour that is even better the next day, so be sure to make plenty. For a real kick, add a teaspoon of harissa paste too. Serve with crusty bread or North African flat breads.

INGREDIENTS

1 onion, chopped

2 garlic cloves, chopped

2 carrots, chopped

1 tbsp ground cumin

1 tsp ground coriander

2 x 400g cans chopped tomatoes

1 vegetable stock cube, made up with 600ml (1 pint) water

1 preserved lemon, plus extra to garnish

3 tbsp chopped fresh coriander, plus extra to garnish

salt and black pepper

a few black olives, chopped, to garnish

olive oil, to garnish

Here's how

Put the chopped onion, garlic and carrots in a large pan on a medium heat and sprinkle with the ground spices.

Add the canned tomatoes and vegetable stock and simmer for 30–40 minutes until the carrots are soft and tender.

Chop the preserved lemon and add most of it to the soup with the 3tbsp coriander. Blend until smooth. Season with salt and pepper to taste.

Ladle the soup into bowls and garnish with the reserved chopped preserved lemon, reserved coriander and the chopped black olives, finishing with a drizzle of olive oil.

My perfect cheese toastie

This recipe is the ultimate in simplicity and comfort food, but don't underestimate it – when it's done right it's the best thing ever. There is something very special about this great combination of different cheeses and onions.

INGREDIENTS

½ white onion

salt and black pepper

2 tbsp oil

100g (3½oz) mature cheese, grated

75g (3oz) hard cow's milk mozzarella, grated

50g (2oz) Parmesan or pecorino, grated

1 red onion

handful of fresh chives

4 spring onions

1 tbsp Dijon or wholegrain mustard

8 slices of good-quality sourdough or bloomer bread

50g (2oz) butter

Here's how

Preheat a non-stick frying pan.

Slice the white onion as thinly as possible and add to the pan with a sprinkle of salt and a drizzle of oil.

Let the onion cook for 15–20 minutes until it has turned golden, sweet and sticky. It might take a while but it's worth it: you could always cook twice as much as you need and keep the rest in the fridge for another day.

Meanwhile put all the grated cheeses in a mixing bowl. Chop the red onion as finely as possible and chop the chives and spring onions. Add them to the grated cheese.

When the cooked onion is golden and sweet, add it to the cheese mixture with the mustard and mix together.

Butter one side of each slice of bread. Turn 4 slices over, and add a generous helping of the cheese mixture. Top with a slice of bread, ensuring the buttered side is uppermost.

Use some kitchen paper to wipe clean the frying pan you cooked the onions in. Preheat the frying pan.

Put two sandwiches at a time into the pan and cook for 4–5 minutes on each side until golden and crisp.

Oriental salmon

Salmon is quick and easy to cook – and it's good for you. I convinced my daughter to eat salmon because it's pink. Young children also like it because it's easy to chew – it's an ideal first food. This dish is a great mix of oriental flavours. Serve with rice or soy-dressed noodles.

INGREDIENTS

1 tbsp sesame oil

4 salmon fillets

2 garlic cloves

6 shallots

5cm (2in) piece of fresh ginger

2 limes

stick of lemongrass

bunch of spring onions

2 red chillies

handful of fresh coriander,
  including the stalks

2 tbsp soy sauce

Here's how

Preheat the oven to 180°C/350°F/Gas Mark 4. Line a baking tray with kitchen foil. Drizzle the sesame oil on to the foil and spread it around.

Lay the salmon pieces on the foil, making sure there is space in between the fillets.

Peel and chop the garlic and shallots. Peel the ginger and slice thinly. Put them all in a mixing bowl.

Cut the limes into quarters and squeeze out the juice into the bowl, then throw in the squeezed-out limes as well – there is still plenty of flavour in them.

Slice the lemongrass finely and chop the spring onions into 2–3cm (¾–1¼in) lengths.

Deseed the chillies and chop them into matchsticks.

Separate the coriander stalks and leaves, reserving the leaves. Chop the stalks and add them to the bowl. Mix together.

Splash the soy sauce all over the salmon and then pile all the flavouring ingredients on top.

Cover with another piece of foil and bake for 25–30 minutes.

Squeeze the lime quarters over the fish and serve scattered with the reserved coriander leaves.

Tip

Get this dish ready in the morning and leave it wrapped up in the fridge until you're ready to cook it.

Chorizo and egg tortilla wrap

Eggs and chorizo are just made for each other and this dish is a chef's favourite – I cook it in my kitchen at work or at home when the boys come round. It's so incredibly easy and versatile – I've even rustled it up over a camp fire.

INGREDIENTS

8 large eggs

salt and black pepper

olive oil, for frying

20 thin slices of ready-sliced chorizo sausage

50g (2oz) Parmesan

4 tortilla wraps

Here's how

Heat an ovenproof frying pan. Whisk together the eggs with a splash of water and season with salt and pepper.

Put a drizzle of oil into the frying pan followed by a quarter of the egg mixture. Lay 5 slices of chorizo sausage on top and let the frittata cook for about 3–4 minutes until cooked.

Preheat the oven to 200°C/400°F/Gas Mark 6 or heat the grill to high.

Grate some Parmesan (or any other similar cheese) on top of the frittata and bang it into the hot oven for 2 minutes or slip it under the grill – or leave the pan on the camp fire for a bit longer.

Slide the frittata on to a tortilla wrap and roll up. Serve to the first hungry person while you rattle off the rest – or keep the wraps warm in the oven.

I'm starving!

My steak sarnie

Who doesn't love a steak sarnie? But anything this simple has to be done well. I always say to my chefs – or anyone else, for that matter – if you are going to cook simply, you must execute it perfectly. Follow my lead on this and you will have the best steak sarnie ever, I promise.

INGREDIENTS

3–4 x 175g (6oz) skirt beef steaks (depending on appetites)

olive oil for drizzling, plus 2 tbsp for salad dressing

salt and black pepper

6 tbsp soured cream

2 tbsp English mustard

2 tbsp creamed horseradish sauce

juice of ½ lemon

1 large ciabatta loaf or 4 individual ones

500g (1lb) mixed salad leaves or rocket

2 tbsp sherry vinegar

Here's how

Season the steaks well with a drizzle of olive oil and salt and pepper on both sides.

Heat a non-stick frying pan. Fry the steaks for 3–4 minutes on each side for medium rare, longer if you prefer your steak well done.

Put the soured cream, mustard, creamed horseradish and lemon juice in a bowl and whisk together.

When the steaks are cooked to your liking, take the pan off the heat and let the steaks rest for a few minutes while you put the sandwiches together.

Cut the loaf or loaves in half and spread both sides generously with the soured-cream mixture. Dress the salad leaves or rocket with the vinegar and olive oil, then place them on top of the bread.

Using a sharp knife, carve the steaks into 1cm (½ in) sticks. Put them in a bowl, otherwise you will lose all the lovely juices.

Lay the beef strips on the sandwich, then you know what to do – tuck in and enjoy my ultimate steak sarnie.

I'm starving!

Mushrooms on toast

Mushrooms on toast for me is a real treat, but only if it's done properly – no soggy wet mushrooms or dry toast. The mushrooms must be cooked perfectly so that all the water within them is cooked out, to leave a wonderful earthy flavour, laced with one of my new favourite ingredients – Worcestershire sauce.

INGREDIENTS

500g (1lb) mushrooms (I like to use chestnut ones)

2 tbsp olive oil

75g (3oz) butter, plus extra

sea salt and black pepper

1 tsp chopped rosemary leaves

1 tsp chopped thyme leaves

2–3 tbsp Worcestershire sauce

4 thick-cut slices of bread for toasting

Here's how

Slice the mushrooms in half. Heat a non-stick frying pan and add the mushrooms cut-side down, along with the olive oil and butter. Season with sea salt and black pepper. The salt helps draw out the moisture from the mushrooms so that they turn a mouth-watering golden colour.

Add the chopped rosemary and thyme.

Turn the mushrooms over when they are golden, and continue to cook for a few more minutes.

Then add a few splashes of Worcestershire sauce – it makes all the difference.

Serve up on hot buttered toast.

Amazing leftover chicken sandwich

What shall we do with the last of yesterday's roast chicken? That's always the question in my house. I'm not that keen on cold chicken sandwiches and I see so many people eating them on a Monday in their packed lunch. If you want to bring a dull sandwich to life, here's how to do it.

INGREDIENTS

juice of ½ a lemon

4 tbsp olive oil

salt and black pepper

leftover roast chicken, ideally 75–125g (3–4oz) per person

12 sunblush tomatoes

16 basil leaves

8 slices of buttered bread or 4 buttered rolls

handful of rocket leaves

Here's how

Put the lemon juice and olive oil in a mixing bowl and whisk together. Season with a little salt and pepper. Add the roast chicken and sunblush tomatoes.

Tear up the basil leaves (if you don't have fresh basil you could always add ½ tsp green pesto from the fridge). Mix the ingredients together so that everything soaks up the dressing and becomes fresh and flavoursome.

Spoon the chicken mixture into the bread rolls or sandwiches, add the rocket, finish with a little more black pepper, and pop it into a lunch box or tuck in straight away.

I'm starving!

Inside-out sandwich

This might sound like a strange way to make a sandwich, but just try it. It could change the way you make sandwiches for ever. As the ham cooks, it acts like a kind of edible shrink wrap, but better still, tastes so good – the juices from the ham soak into the bread and mix with the creamy melted mustardy cheese.

INGREDIENTS
8 slices of bread, bloomer is ideal

25g (1oz) butter

150g (5oz) mature Cheddar

1 tbsp wholegrain mustard

2 tbsp mascarpone

8 slices of air-dried ham

Here's how

Preheat the oven to 180°/350°F/Gas Mark 4.

Butter the bread on one side.

Grate the Cheddar into a bowl and mix with the mustard and mascarpone.

Make 4 sandwiches with the cheese filling, making sure the buttered side of the bread is on the outside.

Wrap each sandwich in ham, like a jacket.

Place the sandwiches on a non-stick baking tray and cook for 20 minutes until crisp.

Goat's cheese and red pepper Spanish-style omelette

If you've got eggs in the fridge, then you've got a meal. Omelettes are great flavour carriers, so all you need to do is crack a couple of eggs and add a few extras. For me, red peppers and goat's cheese make a great combination.

SERVES 1

INGREDIENTS

2 large eggs

2 tbsp milk

salt and black pepper

1 tbsp olive oil

50g (2oz) goat's cheese

sprig of thyme, leaves only

1 roasted red pepper from a jar

a few basil leaves

Here's how

Break the eggs into a small bowl, then add the milk, salt and pepper and whisk with a fork.

Preheat a 20cm (8in) non-stick sauté pan until medium hot and swirl the olive oil in the pan.

Pour in the egg mixture and swirl it in the pan. For a few seconds, gently stir the egg mixture with a heat-resistant rubber spatula (as if you were going to make scrambled eggs) and then swirl the eggs again to make a nice round appearance. Reduce the heat to avoid scorching the base of the omelette. Continue cooking for about 1 minute. The eggs will be set on the bottom, but slightly liquid on top.

Preheat the grill.

Slice the goat's cheese over the centre of the omelette and sprinkle with thyme. Top it off with the roasted pepper. Cook the omelette under the grill for a few minutes to melt the cheese.

To serve, add the fresh basil leaves and a final twist of black pepper.

Tip

Jars of shop-bought roasted peppers preserved in olive oil are the perfect store-cupboard ingredient. Or to roast your own, drizzle a little olive oil over a pepper and place on a baking tray in the oven for 20 minutes at 180°C/350°F/Gas Mark 4.

Tricolore chicken parcels

This is a mid-week favourite in our house: it's a combination of fantastic flavours that you know are going to produce a great meal. Cooking the chicken in a paper parcel ensures all the flavours are kept inside. It's also a forgiving way of cooking as the chicken can sit in the oven and keep warm for 10–20 minutes without drying out.

INGREDIENTS

8 vine tomatoes

4 garlic cloves

16 pitted black olives

handful of basil

4 skinless and boneless chicken breasts

salt and black pepper

oil, for drizzling

zest of 1 lemon

100ml (7fl oz) dry white wine

Here's how

Preheat the oven to 200°C/400°F/Gas Mark 6.

Cut 4 squares of baking parchment approx 50cm (20in) square and lay them on the work surface.

Cut the tomatoes into quarters, divide them between the squares, placing them in the centre of the paper. Crush the garlic and add to the tomatoes. Divide the olives and basil leaves between the 4 portions.

Score the chicken breasts with a sharp knife. Make the cuts approx 1cm (½in) deep to let in lots of flavour. Season the chicken with salt and pepper, then place on top of the tomatoes. Drizzle with a little olive oil and a few rasps of lemon zest.

Fold up the paper to create parcels and transfer them to a large baking tray.

Before you put them in the oven, open the folded parcels slightly and pour a little wine in each: this will create steam and helps all the flavours melt into each other, to make an amazing sauce. Fold the parcels back up to lock in all the flavour and cook for 25–30 minutes.

Easy entertaining

Friends coming round? Don't know what to cook?
No problem! This bunch of recipes will have friends
and family queuing up to be invited back again.
When I have friends over, the last thing I want to
do is spend all my time in the kitchen. Get prepared
in advance and you can relax with your guests. This
is a collection of some of my most successful dishes
that I created for just such occasions. They work for
me and I'm sure they'll work for you, too.

Smoked salmon doughnuts

These tasty little nibbles are a great way to start a dinner party or if you just fancy something light for supper. I've used smoked salmon as I love its flavour. Always remember the finishing touches – a sprinkle of sea salt and a squeeze of lemon make all the difference.

INGREDIENTS

4 egg whites

pinch of sea salt

3 tbsp basil leaves

1 lemon

75g (3oz) smoked salmon, chopped

2 tbsp self-raising flour

vegetable oil, for frying

Here's how

Whisk up the egg whites with a pinch of sea salt until light and fluffy.

Roughly chop the basil leaves and add to the egg whites. Zest the lemon and add the zest to the egg mixture with the chopped smoked salmon.

Fold in the flour carefully so as not to knock any air out of the mixture.

In a large frying pan heat around 5cm (2in) depth of vegetable oil. When it is approximately 170°C/340°F start cooking the doughnuts. Test it by putting your spoon into the oil with a tiny bit of the mixture on, if it starts to crackle then the oil is ready.

Dip a tablespoon into the hot oil then use it to scoop out a generous spoonful of the doughnut mixture and drop it into the oil.

Cook about 4 doughnuts at a time. Turn them over after approximately 45 seconds – they should be golden and crispy – then cook on the remaining side. Remove from the pan and drain them on kitchen paper to absorb excess oil.

If necessary, keep the doughnuts warm in the oven while you cook the rest.

Serve with the lemon you used for the zest, cut into quarters.

Cured ham and capers

This recipe is very simple – it relies on top-quality ingredients and nothing else. It's a real favourite of mine that I like to make when we're on holiday in Tuscany. Failing that, just go shopping in your best Italian deli.

INGREDIENTS

16 slices of cured ham such as prosciutto, Parma, serrano or, even better, cured ham from your local farmer

2 tbsp mini capers

50g (2oz) pecorino

100g (3½oz) rocket

3–4 tbsp good-quality extra-virgin olive oil

black pepper

Here's how

Lay out the ham on a large flat plate. Drain the capers and sprinkle them over the ham.

Using a vegetable peeler, shave the cheese into thin strips and let them drop all over the ham.

Top with the rocket leaves and season with freshly ground black pepper. Dress with extra-virgin olive oil just before serving.

Salmon parcels with pickled fennel and courgette

Cooking fish in a parcel is my favourite technique. It's a great way of packaging up flavours, as well as keeping all the moisture in. You can create all kinds of different combinations – I love pickled fennel with ribbons of courgette.

INGREDIENTS

3 courgettes
4 x 200g (7oz) salmon fillets
75g (3oz) butter
1 lemon

For the pickled fennel

2 fennel bulbs
100g (3½oz) icing sugar
200ml (7fl oz) white wine vinegar
salt and black pepper
1 tbsp fennel seeds

Here's how

First make the pickled fennel. Slice the fennel as thinly as you can.

Put the icing sugar and white wine vinegar in a saucepan and bring to the boil, then add the fennel and turn off the heat.

Season with a little salt and pepper plus the fennel seeds for extra flavour, then put the fennel and pickling liquid in a clean sterile jam jar. You won't need it all for this dish and it will keep in the fridge for about 4 weeks.

Using a vegetable peeler, cut the courgettes into ribbons and put them in a bowl. Add a handful of the pickled fennel and mix together.

Preheat the oven to 180°C/350°F/Gas Mark 4.

Roll out a length of baking parchment over your chopping board. Place a handful of the courgette and fennel mixture in the centre and lay a fillet of salmon on top, and season lightly. Add a knob of butter and a squeeze of lemon. Fold the parchment up to create a parcel. Repeat for the remaining salmon fillets.

Put the foil parcels on a baking tray and cook in the oven for 20 minutes.

Mussels and beer

It's not common knowledge but we produce really good mussels in the UK. We also brew great beer, so it makes perfect sense to put the two together. Mussels are surprisingly easy to cook. Just remember to get your pan hot first, then it's in with the ingredients.

INGREDIENTS

bunch of spring onions

1.75kg (3½lb) mussels

500ml (17fl oz) local beer, light if possible

salt and black pepper

1 tbsp finely chopped thyme, plus extra to garnish

crusty bread, to serve

lemon wedges, to serve

Here's how

Cut the spring onions into 1cm (½ in) long pieces.

Heat a large saucepan for 3–4 minutes on medium heat.

Meanwhile wash the mussels and discard any open ones. Tip the rest into the hot pan, then pour in the beer. Season with salt and pepper, add the thyme and spring onions, give it all a good stir and put the lid on. Turn the heat up to full whack and cook the mussels for 4–5 minutes.

Spoon the mussels into four large warmed bowls, garnish with the remaining thyme and serve with lots of crusty bread and a squeeze of lemon. (Remember to throw away any mussels that haven't opened while cooking.)

Salmon with pistachio and herb crust

Salmon on its own can sometimes be a little dull, but adding some cream cheese and a nutty herb crust turns it into a perfect dinner. I like to serve this dish with new potatoes and maybe some carrots or a dressed green salad.

INGREDIENTS

2 tbsp pistachio nuts

4 salmon fillets with the bones taken out

100g (3½oz) breadcrumbs

2 tbsp parsley

zest of 1 lemon

2–3 tbsp cream cheese

salt and black pepper

olive oil, for drizzling

Here's how

Preheat the oven to 180°C/350°F/Gas Mark 4.

Toast the pistachios in the oven for 10 minutes. Leave the oven on.

Leave the pistachios to cool, then whizz them in a food processor with the breadcrumbs, parsley and lemon zest.

Carefully spread the cream cheese on top of each salmon fillet. Place the fillets on a non-stick baking tray, season with salt and pepper, then top them with plenty of the breadcrumb mixture. Drizzle with a little olive oil to help it crisp up in the oven.

Bake the salmon for 15–20 minutes until it is cooked through.

Melon and mint

You might think I have gone a little bonkers here but, believe me, grating some extra-strong mints over the top of this refreshing melon salad makes all the difference. They add such a freshness to the whole dish – this is a must-try recipe!

INGREDIENTS

1 cantaloupe melon

1 honeydew melon

½ a watermelon

juice of 2 limes

2 tbsp clear runny honey

2 tbsp olive oil (not extra-virgin)

handful of fresh mint

4 extra-strong mints

Here's how

Cut off the top and base of each of the whole melons to make them stand firmly. Using a sharp knife, cut around the melons to remove the skin. Cut the fruit down the middle and remove the seeds if necessary.

Peel and deseed the half watermelon.

Slice all the melons thinly and arrange them on a large serving plate.

In a small bowl mix together the lime juice, honey and olive oil, then pour the dressing over the melon. Chop the fresh mint and scatter it over.

Just before you serve the dish, use a zester or fine grater to grate the extra-strong mints all over the plate of melon.

Sea bass with lime and chilli

This dish was inspired by a fabulous restaurant we visit in East Yorkshire when catching up with friends. I always order it and you can bet everyone round the table ends up tucking in and trying it. Thai food is so fragrant and full flavoured yet comes across as very light. Serve with sticky rice or a carrot, mango, peanut and coriander Thai salad.

INGREDIENTS

50g (2oz) fresh ginger

2 garlic cloves

zest and juice of 4 limes

4 tbsp fish sauce

½ tsp white sugar

2 sticks of lemon grass

2 red chillies, deseeded

8 spring onions

oil, for drizzling

4 whole sea bass, gutted and scaled

2 handfuls of fresh coriander, chopped

lime wedges, to serve

Here's how

Preheat the oven to 200°C/400°F/Gas Mark 6.

Using a fine grater, grate the fresh ginger, garlic and lime zest into a mixing bowl (or you can chop them with a knife if you prefer). Add the lime juice, fish sauce and sugar. Slice the lemon grass and red chillies finely and add to the mixture. Slice the spring onions into 2cm (¾in) long pieces and add to the bowl.

Lay out 4 pieces of foil, approx 60–70cm (24–28in) square. Drizzle some oil in the centre of the foil to stop the fish sticking.

Lay a sea bass in the centre of each foil square and stuff each fish with the ginger and garlic mixture.

Bring up the edges of the foil to keep in the juices, then fold up the foil to seal. Put the parcels on a baking tray and cook for 30 minutes.

When cooked, tear open the parcels and add lots of chopped coriander and a few wedges of lime.

Fougasse

This French-style bread is the ideal recipe for anyone just getting interested in making bread by hand – it's the next step after making a good white loaf. It's great for tearing and sharing with family or friends. Try serving it with air-dried ham or with extra-virgin olive oil with a dash of good aged balsamic vinegar for dipping.

INGREDIENTS

10g (1 heaped tsp) fresh yeast or 5g (½ level tsp) dried yeast

500g (1lb) strong bread flour

10g (1 level tsp) sea salt

350ml (12fl oz) water

Here's how

Rub the fresh yeast into the flour (or mix in the dried yeast). Add the salt and the water. Mix for a couple of minutes until the dough starts to form.

Transfer the dough to a work surface. Continue to mix by stretching out the dough and folding it over on to itself. Keep working it until it comes cleanly away from the work surface and is not sticky.

Lightly flour the work surface, place the dough on the flour and form it into a ball.

Place the dough in a mixing bowl and cover with a tea towel. Rest it for at least an hour. Turn the dough out gently on to a well-floured surface. Be careful not to deflate it; expect it to spread out to cover an area of your work surface about 30cm (1ft) square. Generously flour the top of the dough, cover with a clean tea towel and rest for five minutes.

Using a plastic scraper (or a thin wooden spatula), divide the dough into 2 pieces, then roll them out flat. Using a sharp knife, carefully make 4 or 5 cuts in each piece so that you can stretch it out to look like a leaf. Gently open out the holes with your fingers and shake off the excess flour.

Lift the two loaves on to non-stick baking trays and leave to prove for 30 minutes until they have doubled in size and look lighter and puffed up.

Preheat the oven to 200°C/400°F/Gas Mark 6.

Bake the loaves for 20 minutes until golden and crisp.

Halloumi cheese with roasted sweet potatoes, squash and lime

This is a perfect dish for putting in the middle of the table and letting everybody tuck in. It's a combination of everything you could possible want: sweet and nutty squash, salty crispy cheese, a kick of chilli and a tang of lime.

INGREDIENTS

1 butternut squash

3 medium-sized sweet potatoes

3 tbsp olive oil, plus extra, to drizzle

2 garlic cloves, crushed

salt and black pepper

3 red onions

1 red chilli

1 block of halloumi cheese weighing 250g (8oz)

2 limes, cut into wedges

small handful of coriander

small handful of mint

Here's how

Preheat the oven to 180°C/350°F/Gas Mark 4.

Peel the squash and sweet potatoes and chop to approximately the same size. Throw them in a bowl with the olive oil, crushed garlic cloves and some salt and pepper.

Carefully peel the red onions, making sure you don't cut the roots off, then cut them into quarters – if the roots are intact they won't fall apart while roasting. They should be about the same size as the potatoes and squash.

Spread the vegetables on a large roasting tray and roast for 25–30 minutes.

When the vegetables are cooked, turn the oven off and leave them to keep warm while you do the last bit of cooking.

Remove the seeds and slice the red chilli into thin matchsticks. Chop the coriander.

Cut the halloumi into 1cm (½in) slices and drizzle with a little oil.

Heat a non-stick frying pan and cook the cheese on each side until golden and crisp.

Remove the vegetables from the oven and tip on to a large family-sized plate. Top them with the chilli sticks, slices of cheese and the wedges of lime, then scatter with the coriander and mint leaves.

Make sure everyone helps themselves to a wedge of lime along with the veg – that citrus burst really makes the dish sing!

Tip

Get the dish to the table quickly once you have cooked the cheese – it has a habit of turning chewy if you leave it too long.

Duck breasts with parsnip chips and plum ketchup

You don't need me to tell you that duck and plums work really well together. And autumn is the best time to make this tasty and versatile ketchup using British plums. Put it together with tender duck breasts and some seriously tasty parsnip chips.

INGREDIENTS

4 x 175–200g (6–7oz) duck breasts

salt and black pepper

1 tsp fresh thyme leaves

For the plum ketchup

1kg (2lb) plums, halved and stones removed

handful of sultanas

2 onions, peeled and chopped

600ml (1 pint) white vinegar

250g (8oz) sugar

1 star anise

salt and black pepper

For the parsnip chips

8 medium-sized parsnips, quartered lengthways

3 tbsp olive oil

1 tbsp fresh thyme leaves

salt and black pepper

Here's how

Make the plum ketchup. Put all the ingredients in a large pan and cook on a low heat until the plums are soft and squidgy and the sugar is completely dissolved.

Leave the ketchup to cool a little, then remove the star anise and blend the ketchup until smooth.

Taste the ketchup. If it's too sweet, add a little extra vinegar to balance the flavour. Season if required. Pot the ketchup in clean sterilised jam jars and store in the fridge – it will keep for up to 4 weeks.

Preheat the oven to 180°C/350°F/Gas Mark 4.

Put the parsnip quarters on a large roasting tray and drizzle with the oil. Add the thyme leaves and a little salt and pepper and roast the parsnips for 30 minutes until cooked.

Meanwhile, using a sharp knife, make small cuts in the duck skin approx ½cm (¼in) deep. Season with salt, pepper and a little chopped thyme.

Cook the duck breasts skin-side down in a non-stick frying pan until the skin is golden and crispy – about 4–5 minutes.

Flip the breasts over and cook them for a further 3–4 minutes on a low heat – or you can put them in the tray with the parsnips to finish cooking for about 10 minutes.

Coq à la bière

Coq au vin is a great dish and really easy to knock up for the family. But in the UK we can be a bit stuck for our lack of good home-produced red wine. One day when I was planning to make *coq au vin*, all I could find in the cupboard was English beer so that went in instead. It worked so well that I've been making it ever since. Here's my recipe for *coq à la bière*.

INGREDIENTS

8 chicken thighs

salt and black pepper

sprigs of thyme

sprig of rosemary

8 shallots, chopped

4–6 rashers of dry cured smoked bacon

200g (7oz) button mushrooms, halved

1 garlic bulb

1 tbsp chopped rosemary

6 juniper berries

1 tbsp chopped fresh sage

500ml (17fl oz) bottle of your local beer

1 chicken stock cube

Here's how

Make small cuts in the chicken thighs, piercing through the skin, to allow lots of flavour to penetrate. Put them in a mixing bowl with the salt, pepper, thyme and rosemary sprigs. Leave to marinate for a couple of hours.

Preheat the oven to 180°C/350°F/Gas Mark 4.

Put the chicken thighs in a deep roasting tray with the shallots, bacon and mushrooms and cook in the oven for 20 minutes to get some good colour. Remove from the oven. Reduce the heat to 160°C/325°F/Gas Mark 3.

This is where we start building up the flavour. Cut the garlic bulb into horizontal slices. (I know it sounds like a lot of garlic, but it calms down and smooths out to give a wonderful sweet rich taste.) Chuck in the chopped rosemary, juniper berries and chopped sage. Pour in the beer and add the chicken stock cube. Cover the roasting tin with foil and put it back in the oven for 1 hour.

Tip

Use a good-quality stock cube – it really makes all the difference.

Pecorino cheese with toasted walnuts, pear and honey

I love this dish! It's another easy combination of simple ingredients, with just a few little tweaks to bring out the best of each of them. I always cook this for my wife's family, as it brings back great memories of our holidays together in Tuscany.

INGREDIENTS

handful of walnuts
4 tbsp olive oil
sprigs of rosemary
3 tbsp honey
1 tsp sea salt flakes
3 pears
juice of ½ a lemon
150g (5oz) pecorino
handful of rocket

Here's how

Toast the walnuts in a non-stick frying pan with 2 tbsp of the olive oil, on a medium heat. When they start to crackle a little and turn golden brown, strip the rosemary leaves from the stem and throw them in with the nuts.

Remove the pan from the heat and add 1 tbsp of the honey and season with the sea salt flakes.

Leave the nuts to cool while you prepare the pears. Mix the remaining olive oil, lemon juice and remaining honey together to make a dressing.

Cut the pears into quarters and remove the core. Slice each quarter thinly – or, if you want a bit of crunch, make the slices thicker.

Add the pears to the dressing, making sure they all get coated.

Slice the cheese and spread it out on a plate. Top with the pears and toasted walnuts, scatter with rocket and serve.

Beef nachos

Nachos are a great way to share food with friends or family. But how often have you ordered nachos when eating out and found all the chips at the top have cheese on while the bottom of the bowl is dry as a bone? Use a large flat plate and every chip will get a little bit of everything.

INGREDIENTS

For the nachos

4–6 x 23cm (9in) tortilla wraps

3 tbsp oil

1 tsp cayenne pepper

For the salsa

1 large red pepper

1 large yellow pepper

oil, to drizzle

1 medium red onion

juice and zest of 1 lime

1 tsp salt

2 large fresh tomatoes

1 red chilli

4 tbsp ketchup

salt and black pepper, to taste

handful of fresh coriander

For the dip

200g (7oz) tub crème fraîche

juice of 1 lime

black pepper

For the steak

2 steaks, either rump or sirloin

1 tbsp oil

salt and cracked black pepper

To serve

a handful of grated hard cow's milk mozzarella cheese

lemon wedges

Here's how

Preheat the oven to 160°C/325°F/Gas Mark 3.

Pile the tortilla wraps on top of each other and cut through the stack, cutting them into 8 portions. Put them in a bowl and drizzle with the oil, followed by the cayenne pepper Stir the chips around to make sure they get covered in a little of the oil and pepper.

Spread the chips on a baking tray, making sure they are not sitting on top of each other. Bake for 20 minutes until crisp.

Meanwhile, make the salsa. Drizzle the peppers with a little olive oil and cook in the oven for 30 minutes until roasted and soft. Chop the red onion as finely as possible and place in a bowl with the lime zest and juice, and sprinkle with the salt. Leave the onion to soften for 10 minutes or so while you chop and deseed the tomatoes.

Peel, skin and chop the roasted peppers once cool enough to handle. Add the chopped tomatoes to the onions, followed by the roasted peppers.

Chop the chilli and add to the salsa with the ketchup. If you like things really hot, add the chilli seeds as well. Taste the salsa and season accordingly if required. Add the chopped coriander and set to one side.

To make the dip, mix together the crème fraîche and lime juice and season with a touch of black pepper.

To cook the steak, preheat a grill pan until it is smoking hot.

Drizzle a little oil on to both sides of the steaks and season with salt and cracked black pepper. Cook them on one side for 2–3 minutes, turn over and cook for a further 2 minutes for medium-rare meat (or longer if you prefer your meat to be cooked right through).

When the steaks are cooked, leave to rest for a few minutes then slice them up into thin strips.

Put the tortilla chips on a large heatproof plate in a single layer. Sprinkle with grated mozzarella then scatter the strips of steak all over, followed by spoonfuls of salsa. Place in a hot oven or under a preheated grill for a few minutes to melt the cheese. Serve with the dip and lemon wedges.

Vanilla and blackberry vodka for the grownups

This is one for the adults. It's a great gift for any foodie friends: make it in September and it will be ready by December. I'm not a big fan of spirits – give me a cold beer any day – but a shot of this served neat, or poured over ice with some lemonade, is a real cool crowd pleaser.

INGREDIENTS

500ml (17fl oz) bottle of vodka

1 vanilla pod

75g (3oz) caster sugar

20 fresh ripe blackberries

Here's how

First pour out 100ml (3½fl oz) vodka from the bottle – store it in an empty container or make a round of vodka and tonics.

Cut the vanilla pod down the middle lengthways to reveal the seeds. Put it in the bottle, along with the sugar and blackberries. Replace the lid and shake the living daylights out of the bottle to mix all the ingredients together.

Now you can do one of two things. If you are a patient person, leave the bottle in the cupboard for 8 weeks and allow the flavours to mature. Or, if you are anything like me, and you want to drink it ASAP, this method is for you. Make sure the lid is screwed on as tightly as possible, then put the bottle in the dishwasher and turn it on at your usual setting.

The heat of the washing cycle will speed up the infusion of flavours.

When the cycle has finished, place the bottle in the fridge or freezer to cool.

Pork rillette

I love the versatility of pork – you can do so many different things with it. Here's my recipe for rillette, a wonderful, rich, flavoursome French pâté with a coarse texture. It tastes even better if you can leave it for a few days. This is a great dish to serve for a dinner party or just a nice supper for two in front of the fire.

INGREDIENTS

250g (8oz) butter

1 garlic clove, crushed

100g (3½oz) smoked streaky bacon or pancetta

2 onions, sliced

400ml (14fl oz) dry white wine

sprig of rosemary

sprig of thyme

juice of 1 lemon

1kg (2lb) pork shoulder, diced

salt and black pepper

2 tbsp mini capers

handful of parsley, chopped

Here's how

Melt the butter in a large saucepan – use one that has a lid. Add the garlic, bacon or pancetta and onions and cook until softened. Add the wine, rosemary, thyme and lemon juice.

Then add the pork and cook on a low heat for a couple of hours, leaving the lid half over the pan so that it is less likely to boil over.

The pork should be mega-tender and fall apart when you lift it out of the pan. Remove the pan from the heat and pour the contents through a sieve or colander, making sure you save the cooking juices.

Discard the herb sprigs and put the pork in a mixing bowl. The meat will be really tender so you should be able to break it down using just a spoon.

Season with a little salt and pepper, add the capers and parsley then mix together.

Transfer the meat into clean sterile jam jars or into a bowl and press it down to compact it – to make a coarse pâté. Pour over some of the reserved juices and leave to soak in.

After 10 minutes the juices will have found their way down to the bottom of the jar or bowl. Repeat the process until the juices cover the pork.

Keep the pâté in the fridge until you are ready to use it.

Allow 30 minutes or so before serving for it to warm up to room temperature, as it will taste better than straight from the fridge.

My best ever cheesecake

I love a great cheesecake, but you rarely come across a good one in a restaurant, so I tend to make it myself. Cheesecake is my guilty pleasure, so here's my recipe which I've developed and perfected over the years. Be warned – it's not for the faint-hearted.

INGREDIENTS

200g (7oz) digestive biscuits

50g (2oz) butter, melted

750g (1½lb) full-fat Philadelphia cream cheese

225g (7½oz) caster sugar

3 tbsp corn flour

2 vanilla pods, seeds only

few drops vanilla extract

2 tbsp lemon juice

2 eggs, beaten

250ml (8fl oz) double cream

punnet of fresh blackberries, to serve

Here's how

Place the biscuits in a blender and process to a crumb consistency. Mix with the melted butter.

Push the mixture firmly into a lined 20–24cm (8–9½in) round cake tin. Refrigerate to set.

Preheat the oven to 180°C/350°F/Gas Mark 4.

Combine the cream cheese, sugar, corn flour, vanilla seeds, vanilla extract and lemon juice in a food mixer, using a beater attachment and the slowest setting. Mix until smooth and thick.

Add the eggs and cream and continue to mix until very thick. Spoon into the prepared cake tin on top of the biscuit base and bake for 45 minutes.

Leave the cheesecake to cool. Once cool, lift it out of the tin and top with fresh blackberries.

Weekends

For me the weekends are so special. If you've been at work all week, you'll treasure spending two whole days together as a family. It's time to really enjoy yourselves, with great food for everyone to tuck into. This chapter is packed full of recipes for when time is not an issue – slow-cooked dishes, roasts and bakes. These dishes are best served chilled – I'm not talking about the temperature, I'm referring to your state of mind!

Roast pork with fennel and apple sauce

I discovered this fennel and pork combo in a Tuscan food market many years ago. Every market has what we would probably call a hog-roast stall where you can buy wonderful slices of roast pork that has been seasoned with fennel, rosemary and garlic. So I've combined apple and fennel together to make a wonderful accompaniment to the popular Sunday roast.

INGREDIENTS

2.25kg (5lb) pork loin with rind on

2 tbsp olive oil

2 tbsp sea salt

4 onions

sprig of rosemary

For the sauce

2 fennel bulbs

1kg (2lb) cooking apples

5 tbsp cider vinegar

1 tbsp fennel seeds

2 tbsp caster sugar

1 tsp salt

Here's how

Preheat the oven to 220°C/425°F/Gas Mark 7.

Lightly score the pork rind using a sharp knife (or ask your butcher or supermarket meat counter to do this for you).

Drizzle the olive oil over the pork and massage into the skin. Sprinkle with the sea salt. Chop the onions roughly and sit them on the bottom of a roasting tray with the sprig of rosemary. Lay the pork on top and cook for 30 minutes, then reduce the oven temperature to 190°C/375°F/Gas Mark 5, pour in 1.2 litres (2 pints) of water and cook for a further 2 hours.

Meanwhile make the sauce. Chop the fennel bulbs in half and remove and discard the tough central core. Dice the rest as finely as possible. Peel, core and slice the cooking apples.

Put the fennel and apple in a large pan and cook over a medium heat for 5 minutes, then add the vinegar, fennel seeds, sugar and a pinch of salt. Continue to cook for a further 30 minutes until the apples have broken down and the fennel is soft.

Taste to see whether the sauce is sweet enough or sharp enough – you want a nice balance of both to cut through the richness of the pork.

When the pork is cooked remove from the roasting tray and allow to rest for 15 minutes in a warm place before carving.

Tip

This sauce also works really well as a chutney, so why not make a bit extra? I serve roast veg with the pork. I like to cut carrots and parsnips lengthways into quarters, add some onion chunks, drizzle the lot with olive oil and season with sea salt, black pepper and thyme and roast for 40 minutes.

Sausage and sage meatloaf

I think it's time to bring the meatloaf back to the family table. It's the type of dish you can turn into a family favourite by adding your own little touches. In my version I've added some sage, mustard and honey to boost the flavour. Now I have to confess that eating meatloaf cold straight from the fridge late at night is one of my vices – well, we all have our weaknesses.

INGREDIENTS

625g (1¼lb) sausagemeat

8 sage leaves

1 medium onion, chopped finely

150g (5oz) breadcrumbs

2 eggs

2 tbsp milk

salt and black pepper

1 tbsp honey

1 tbsp wholegrain mustard

Here's how

Preheat the oven to 180°C/350°F/Gas Mark 4.

Place all the ingredients in a large mixing bowl and mix thoroughly – it's best to use your hands to do this.

Transfer the mixture to a 1kg (2lb) loaf tin and pat down until the surface is level. Cover the top with an oiled piece of greaseproof paper.

Bake in the oven for 1 hour 20 minutes or until the meatloaf is cooked through. Leave to cool slightly before turning out and slicing.

Honey and mustard new potatoes

When you cook new potatoes they soak up flavour like a sponge, so I always add a dressing as soon as they are drained. What better combination than honey, mustard and vinegar to create a tangy yet sweet dressing. Serve hot or leave to cool for a knock-out potato salad.

INGREDIENTS

500g (1lb) new potatoes

salt

2 tbsp balsamic vinegar

4 tbsp olive oil

2 tbsp wholegrain mustard

2 tbsp runny honey

sprigs of thyme

Here's how

If the new potatoes are large, slice them diagonally – this increases the surface area to allow more flavour in. Leave small potatoes whole. Cook the potatoes in boiling salted water until tender.

While they are cooking mix together the vinegar, olive oil, mustard and honey to make a dressing.

When the potatoes are cooked, drain them in a colander and tip them back into the pan they were cooked in. Add the thyme and pour in the dressing, giving the pan a shake so that all the potatoes are coated.

Gammon with a spicy honey glaze

Ham with HP sauce is one of my childhood favourites, so when I put together this sweet and sticky glaze for a nice joint of gammon it had to have HP in it. Mixed with honey, HP balances the sweetness with its spicy tang, which is boosted by the cloves.

INGREDIENTS

3kg (6½lb) gammon joint

5 tbsp HP or brown sauce

4 tbsp honey

10 cloves or more, to taste

Here's how

Put the gammon in a large pan and cover it with water. Bring up to the boil then let the gammon simmer so that the water is just bubbling away. Leave it to cook for 2 hours.

When the gammon is cooked remove it from the water carefully.

Preheat the oven to 180°C/375°F/Gas Mark 4.

Using a sharp knife, cut away and discard the skin from the gammon joint.

In a mixing bowl, whisk together the brown sauce and honey.

Press the cloves into the meat all over the joint. Pour over half of the glaze and roast the joint in the oven for 25 minutes.

Remove from the oven and re-glaze with the last of the mixture then return the joint to the oven for a further 10 minutes.

When the meat comes out of the oven you'll be desperate to cut yourself a slice off the end where no one can see – but please be careful, as it will be really, really hot, and yummy.

Duck and root vegetables

Roasted British root vegetables turn fabulously crispy, sweet and sticky – and give chips a run for their money any day. They work brilliantly with some simple duck breasts. Cook them all together to make an interesting one-pot dish packed full of flavour.

INGREDIENTS

4 medium parsnips, quartered lengthways

4 medium carrots, quartered lengthways

2 beetroot, quartered

2 red onions, quartered

8 small or 4 large shallots, peeled and cut in half

4–5 sprigs of thyme, plus 1 tbsp chopped leaves for the dressing

3 tbsp olive oil

4 x 175–200g (6–7oz) duck breasts

salt and black pepper

juice of ½ a lemon

2 tbsp runny honey

Here's how

Preheat the oven to 180°C/375°F/Gas Mark 4.

Put the vegetables in a roasting tray and add the thyme sprigs and olive oil and roast for 30 minutes.

Meanwhile heat a non-stick frying pan and season the duck breasts with salt and pepper on both sides then lay the breasts skin-side down in the frying pan and cook until the skin turns a wonderful golden colour – about 4–5 minutes.

Then finish cooking them in the roasting tray with the vegetables for the final 15 minutes.

While the duck and vegetables are cooking, make the dressing. Mix together the lemon juice, honey, chopped thyme, salt and pepper.

Pour the dressing over the cooked vegetables, mixing them carefully so that they get covered with the dressing.

Chicken mole

This is my interpretation of a classic Mexican dish. It's not the most authentic version around, but for me it really represents what Mexican food is all about. Chocolate is a key ingredient but it has to be dark chocolate for its rich bitter flavour.

INGREDIENTS

1 tsp chilli

1 tbsp cumin

1 tsp coriander

1 tsp paprika

3 garlic cloves, chopped

3 tbsp oil

juice of 1 lime

8 chicken thighs

For the sauce

2 x 400g cans chopped tomatoes

500ml (17fl oz) bottle of light beer (Spanish or Mexican is ideal)

2 tbsp tomato purée

75g (3oz) bitter dark chocolate

1 fresh red chilli

1 chicken stock cube

To serve

salt and black pepper

handful of fresh coriander, chopped

1 fresh green chilli or jalapeno chilli from a jar, sliced

lime wedges

Here's how

Put the chilli, cumin, coriander and paprika in a mixing bowl with the chopped garlic, oil and lime juice.

Using a sharp knife make six cuts in each chicken thigh, piercing through the skin, to allow the flavours to penetrate the flesh. Add them to the spice mixture, cover the bowl with clingfilm and leave to marinate for at least 2–3 hours.

Preheat the oven to 180°C/350°F/Gas Mark 4.

Put the marinated chicken thighs in a deep roasting tray and cook for 30 minutes, to allow the skin to crisp up a little.

Meanwhile mix together the ingredients for the sauce. Pour the sauce over the chicken and return to the oven for a further 30–40 minutes.

Taste for seasoning before serving and add salt and pepper if required. Scatter with the coriander and chilli and serve with wedges of lime.

Italian-style roast chicken

This is simply a dish that reminds me of Tuscany, with that heart-warming smell of roast chicken floating through the house – it's the sort of memory that stays with you for ever. Slow-cooked juicy fennel with crisp pancetta, all served up with succulent roast chicken – I'm getting hungry just thinking about it. Serve with roasted or boiled new potatoes.

INGREDIENTS

1.5–2kg (3–4lb) free-range chicken, preferably organic

1 lemon

2 sprigs of thyme

1 garlic bulb, cut in half horizontally

2 bulbs of fennel

200ml (7fl oz) dry white wine

3 tbsp olive oil

sea salt and black pepper

4 slices of pancetta

Here's how

Preheat the oven to 200°C/400°F/Gas Mark 6.

Cut the lemon in half. Put a sprig of thyme into each lemon half and place them inside the cavity of the chicken with the garlic bulb.

Cut the fennel bulbs into quarters, reserving some of the fronds for a garnish, and put them in the roasting tray with the wine.

Put the chicken on top and pour over the oil. Season the chicken generously with sea salt and black pepper.

Roast the chicken for the first 30 minutes at 200°C/400°F/Gas Mark 6, then turn the heat down to 160–180°C/320–350°F/Gas Mark 3–4.

After 1 hour take the chicken out of the oven and cover the breast area with the slices of pancetta. Return it to the oven for a further 30 minutes. The juices should run clear when you pierce the thigh with a skewer.

Turn off the oven and let the bird rest in the residual heat for at least 10 minutes. Remove from the oven, then carve. Chop the pancetta. Serve the chicken on a large platter with the braised fennel and pour the pan juices over the top. Scatter with the pancetta and reserved fennel fronds.

BBQ pork

Belly pork is an all-time favourite of mine. It has so much flavour, plus it's a forgiving cut of meat as it's not easy to over-cook. Just start it at a high temperature, then turn it down to cook for a few hours until tender and melt in the mouth. This recipe was inspired by a trip to the USA, when I was asked to be a judge at a world barbecue championship in Lake Placid, upstate New York. The blend of flavours is sweet and smoky, with just a hint of aniseed that works so well with pork.

INGREDIENTS

2.5kg (5lb) belly of pork

2–3 tbsp olive oil

2 tbsp sea salt

2 onions

2 apples

1 star anise or 1 tsp Chinese five spice

2 tbsp maple syrup

2 tbsp ketchup

2 tbsp brown sauce

2 tbsp dark soy sauce

Here's how

Preheat the oven to 220°C/425°F/Gas Mark 7. Using a sharp knife, cut into the skin of the pork. Make around 10 cuts about 1cm (½in) deep, so that the flavour can soak right into the centre of the meat.

Dry the skin using kitchen paper, as this will help it form some serious crackling – when you cook belly pork, crackling is what it's all about. Drizzle the oil on to the pork and rub it into the skin so it becomes shiny. Season well with sea salt flakes, opening up each cut to make sure some of the salt has got into the meat.

Chop the onions and apples into chunks and put them in a roasting tray.

Sit the pork on top, skin-side up and cook for 20–30 minutes until the skin starts to crisp up.

Turn the oven down to 150°C/300°F/Gas Mark 2 and cook for 2–3 hours until the pork is tender.

While the pork is cooking, make the barbecue glaze. Crush the star anise, if using, with a pestle and mortar. Mix the star anise or five-spice powder with the maple syrup, ketchup, brown sauce and soy sauce.

When the pork is tender and the skin is crispy – after 2–3hrs – brush it with the sauce, making sure it gets into the cuts in the skin.

Put the pork back in the oven for 20–30 minutes so the sauce caramelises and becomes sweet and sticky.

When the pork is ready, please, please rest it before carving. Take it out of the oven, cover with a sheet of foil then place a tea towel over the top to keep it warm. When you have set the table and got everything else ready for your meal, then – and only then – cut the pork into thick slices and chop the crackling into pieces.

Leftovers

Leftover belly pork makes a fantastic dish with cider, apples and black pudding: see page 120.

Beef stifado

I have great memories of Greek food from family holidays and this dish was probably one of the first real foreign foods I tried. The slow cooking method is typically Greek – the dish becomes more intense and flavoursome as the day goes on. It is bold and gutsy and can be enjoyed straight from oven to table or taken to work in a flask. The only thing that would make this dish any better would be to eat it sitting outside watching a Mediterranean sunset.

INGREDIENTS

3 tbsp plain flour

salt and black pepper

1 beef Oxo cube

2kg (4lb) shin of beef, diced into 5cm (2in) chunks

2–3 tbsp olive oil

8 small shallots, peeled (or 2 medium onions, chopped)

1 garlic bulb

6 juniper berries

1 cinnamon stick

200ml (7fl oz) red wine

1 x 400g can chopped tomatoes

300ml (½ pint) beef stock

Here's how

Tip the flour out on to a plate and season with salt and pepper. Crumble the Oxo cube into the flour to help give a boost of beefy flavour.

Roll the beef chunks in the flour, ensuring they are evenly coated.

Preheat a non-stick pan. Add the oil and cook the pieces of beef until they are golden and a little crispy. Do this in batches of 3–4 pieces at a time so the pan does not lose its heat.

When all the chunks of beef are cooked on the outside, put them in a slow cooker or a casserole dish.

Add the peeled shallots. Cut the garlic bulb in half horizontally and add to the pan.

Using the back of a large knife or a rolling pin, crush the juniper berries and add to the beef. Add the cinnamon, red wine, chopped tomatoes and beef stock.

Cover and cook for 8 hours on medium if using a slow cooker or for at least 4 hours in the oven at 160°C/325°F/Gas Mark 3.

The best way to check whether the beef is cooked and tender is to lift out a spoonful and press a chunk with your finger. If the beef breaks open, then it is tender. Taste the sauce and season with salt and pepper if required.

Leftovers

Any leftovers make a fantastic filling for a pie or Cornish-style pasty.

Tip

Vary the recipe by using a bottle of strong local beer instead of wine and adding some chopped carrots along with the shallots; see photograph on page 4.

Roasted chicken legs with lemon, garlic and croutons

This is a firm family favourite. It's easy to make and reasonably priced – in fact, it doesn't work as well with breast so it's a perfect excuse to buy the cheaper leg portions. Legs and thighs also have a lot more flavour. Add the roughly chopped croutons and they'll crisp up beautifully in the chicken juices and the yummy sticky brown bits you get from a roast. Not only will everybody lick their plates, they'll want to lick the roasting tray too!

INGREDIENTS

4 chicken legs

4 chicken thighs

1 garlic bulb

sprig of rosemary

1 lemon, zested and cut into quarters

salt and black pepper

2–3 tbsp olive oil

8–12 chunks of bread, torn up

Here's how

Preheat the oven to 180˚C/375˚F/Gas Mark 4.

Using a sharp knife, slash the chicken down to the bone. This will allow more flavour to penetrate and it will help it cook a little quicker – always helpful when you have a hungry family in front of you.

Cut the bulb of garlic in half horizontally and place in a bowl. Chop the rosemary and add to the bowl, followed by the lemon zest and quarters. Add some salt and pepper and pour in the olive oil.

Put the chicken pieces in the bowl and rub them around, making sure they get covered in all the flavourings. Then tip them out into a roasting tray and cook in the oven for 30 minutes. Take the roasting tray out of the oven and add the torn-up bread.

Give it a stir around, then return the tray to the oven for 10–15 minutes.

Spiced venison stew

We don't cook nearly enough venison in the UK. It's not just for special occasions – you can pretty much do anything with venison that you can do with beef. It's a great meat – free range with lots of flavour – that lends itself to warming winter dishes like this stew.

INGREDIENTS

400g (13oz) venison steaks, cut into chunks

1 leek, thinly sliced

2 carrots, thinly sliced

10 shallots

small handful of rosemary

small handful of thyme, plus extra for garnish

2 bay leaves

1 tbsp coriander seeds

1 bottle red wine

100ml (3½fl oz) sherry vinegar

6 tbsp olive oil

1 cinnamon stick

3 juniper berries

2 garlic cloves

2 cloves

100g (3½oz) dark chocolate, grated

salt and black pepper

Here's how

Place the venison in a large non-reactive bowl. Mix together the leek, carrots, shallots, rosemary, thyme, bay leaves, coriander seeds, red wine and sherry vinegar.

Pour the mixture over the venison and leave to marinate for 12 hours in the fridge.

Remove the meat and vegetables from the marinade using a slotted spoon. Reserve the marinade. Heat 3 tbsp of the olive oil in a frying pan over a medium heat and fry the venison for 3–4 minutes, until browned all over.

Heat the remaining olive oil in a separate pan large enough to hold all the ingredients and fry the vegetables lightly for 3–4 minutes. Add the meat to the vegetables in the pan.

Snap the cinnamon stick in half. Crush the juniper berries with the back of a knife to release the flavour. Crush the garlic. Add the flavourings to the pan with the 2 cloves.

Stir in the marinade and bring to the boil. Turn down the heat and stir in the grated chocolate. Season to taste with salt and freshly ground black pepper, cover and cook over a low heat for 3 hours. Serve immediately, garnished with the extra thyme.

Roast chicken and gnocchi soup

I came up with this recipe as a way of using up small quantities of leftovers. Roasting the chicken carcass a second time really brings out the flavour. Adding gnocchi to the broth makes it more of a meal. Serve with lots of nice crusty French bread.

INGREDIENTS

leftover chicken carcass

2 tbsp olive oil

1.2 litres (2 pints) chicken stock

100ml (3½fl oz) dry white wine

½ a lemon

1 leek, chopped

1 onion, chopped

6 sprigs of fresh thyme, leaves stripped and chopped

sprig of rosemary, leaves stripped and chopped

500g (1lb) shop-bought gnocchi

salt and black pepper

Here's how

Preheat the oven to 180°C/350°F/Gas Mark 4. Remove any meat left on the chicken carcass and keep it to one side.

Put the carcass in a casserole dish, drizzle with the olive oil and cook in the oven for 30 minutes until the carcass becomes golden and crisp.

Add the stock, wine, lemon, chopped leek, onion and herbs to the casserole and put the lid on or cover it with foil, to keep in all the flavour. Reduce the heat to 160°C/325°F/Gas Mark 3 and return the soup to the oven for 45 minutes. Add the gnocchi and the leftover meat and return to the oven for a further 10 minutes.

To serve, carefully remove the chicken carcass, taste and season the soup if necessary, before ladling it into bowls.

Chorizo and roasted pepper sandwich with soured cream

I was introduced to a farmer in Cumbria who makes his own chorizo sausages, so I came up with this combination to enjoy in a sandwich – the peppers are perfectly partnered up with the chorizo and the soured cream just seems to bring it all together nicely.

INGREDIENTS

3 peppers (I use a mixture of colours)

2 garlic cloves

2 tbsp olive oil

8 fresh chorizo-style sausages

4 bread rolls of your choice

soured cream

handful of fresh coriander

handful of salad leaves

1 lime

Here's how

Preheat the oven to 180°C/350°F/Gas Mark 4.

Deseed and chop the peppers. Crush the garlic. Put the peppers and garlic in a roasting tray and drizzle with the olive oil. Roast in the oven for 10 minutes.

Take the tray out of the oven and add the chorizo sausages. Give the tray a good shake then return to the oven for another 20 minutes until the sausages are cooked and all those amazing flavours have mixed together.

Serve up in bread rolls with lots of soured cream, fresh coriander and some salad leaves.

Finish with a squeeze of lime to cut the richness of the peppers and sausage.

Rainy days

Baking is a British institution – we love it. And there is no better way to keep kids amused on a rainy day than baking something yummy in the kitchen. My daughter Poppy is never happier than when she is standing on a chair with her apron on, baking with me or her mum. In this chapter I'm bringing some great British tea-time treats back into the limelight. I think I might even have improved on classics such as custard creams and bourbon biscuits, simply because these are home-made – always best, in my opinion.

Lakeland gingerbread

I live in the Lake District and it's famous for gingerbread. In my opinion the best is Sarah Nelson's from the Grasmere Gingerbread Shop – if you are ever in the area, get yourself in the queue. I have spent years looking into how they make their distinctive gingerbread and pestered them to tell me the family secret. Not surprisingly they won't, so here is my interpretation – it's not the same but it tastes great, as I use three types of ginger to create a really original flavour.

INGREDIENTS

175g (6oz) plain white flour

75g (3oz) brown wholemeal flour

75g (3oz) porridge oats

¾ tsp bicarbonate of soda

1½ tsp ground ginger

275g (9oz) butter

275g (9oz) soft brown sugar

1 thumb-sized piece of fresh ginger

3 pieces of candied ginger, about 4–5cm (1½–2in) each

Here's how

Preheat the oven to 160°C/325°F/ Gas Mark 3. Grease a shallow 35cm (14in) square tin.

In a bowl, combine the flours, oats, bicarbonate of soda and ground ginger – or place in a food processor and pulse to mix together.

Cut the butter into small pieces and rub into the dry ingredients until the mixture resembles breadcrumbs – you can do this in the processor too.

Stir in the sugar.

Peel the fresh ginger and dice into tiny pieces, and add to the mixture. Dice the candied ginger into tiny pieces, too, and add these.

Mix thoroughly, then press the mixture firmly into the tin, pressing down with a floured fork. Bake for 20–30 minutes, until pale brown. Cut into squares while still warm and leave to cool in the tin. Store in an airtight container – it keeps very well.

Iced lemon buns

Iced buns are a childhood favourite of mine: I remember queueing up in the local bakery for them. I have created a recipe that reminds me of the same treat, but using a brioche dough. I think it's a great improvement and it works really well, especially combined with a sweet yet tangy icing that leaves you wanting more.

MAKES 6–8 BUNS, DEPENDING ON SIZE

INGREDIENTS

450g (14oz) strong white flour

7g sachet of dried yeast

4 tbsp sugar

125g (4oz) butter

2 handfuls of mixed dried fruit

zest and juice of 1 lemon

3 large eggs

250ml (8fl oz) milk

200g (7oz) icing sugar

Here's how

Mix together the flour, yeast, sugar and butter. Add the mixed fruit and lemon zest.

Mix the eggs and milk together and pour into the flour mixture a little at a time and mix until you have a bread dough consistency.

Transfer the dough on to a lightly floured work surface and knead it for 5 minutes by stretching the dough away from you, then folding it back over on itself. Keep kneading the dough until it becomes smooth and manageable.

Put the dough back in the mixing bowl, cover with a damp tea towel and leave to rest for 30–40 minutes. It should double in size.

When the dough is light and fluffy, scoop it back out and knead for a further 2 minutes.

Divide the dough into 6–8 portions. Roll them into balls by putting a piece of dough in one hand, bringing your other hand together to squash it, then rolling it into a smooth ball between your palms.

Place the rolls on a baking tray and leave to prove and double in size again, for about 30 minutes.

Preheat the oven to 200°C/400°F/Gas Mark 6.

Bake the rolls for 20 minutes until golden.

Leave the rolls to cool while you make the icing. Mix together the icing sugar and lemon juice to form a thick smooth paste.

When the rolls are cool, spoon over the icing and leave to set (if you can wait that long).

Mocha whirls

This recipe is very close to my heart – I have spent years trying to perfect it. I feel there is truly nothing better to be enjoyed with a smooth well-made flat white coffee than a mocha whirl. Be sure to use a bitter dark chocolate to balance the brioche dough and the coffee icing.

INGREDIENTS

400g (13oz) strong white flour

½ tsp salt

125g (4oz) butter, diced

7g sachet of dried yeast

3 tbsp caster sugar

4 eggs

1½–2 tbsp milk

100g (3½oz) bitter dark
   chocolate

1 tbsp double-strength coffee

100g (3½oz) icing sugar

Here's how

Make the brioche dough. Put the flour, salt and butter in a mixing bowl.

Mix together the yeast, sugar, eggs and milk in a measuring jug.

Pour the liquid into the dry ingredients and, using your hands, mix together until it forms a smooth dough. Transfer the brioche on to a lightly floured work surface and knead for a few minutes until it becomes silky smooth and easy to move about.

Put the dough back in the mixing bowl, cover with a damp tea towel and leave to prove for 30 minutes, until it's doubled in size.

Once the dough has proved, scoop it out on to a lightly floured worktop. Roll it into a rectangle approximately 1cm (½in) thick using a rolling pin.

Break up the chocolate into small chunks and scatter them evenly all over the dough.

Roll the dough towards you like a Swiss roll. Start from the side furthest away from you and roll it up as tightly as possible.

Using a sharp knife, cut the roll into 3cm (1¼in) slices.

Lay them flat on a non-stick baking tray and leave to prove for 20–30 minutes so that they double in size.

Preheat the oven to 190°C/375°F/Gas Mark 5. Bake the whirls for 20 minutes until golden and doubled again in size.

When they have cooled a little, mix together the coffee and icing sugar until smooth, then drizzle all over the whirls.

My oat biscuits

When I bought a packet of Hobnobs in the supermarket, I thought it would be great if I could actually make them myself. So here's my recipe – I have to admit I think my biscuits blow the shop-bought ones out of the water. Once you've tried them you won't go back.

MAKES APPROX 65 BISCUITS

INGREDIENTS
500g (1lb) self-raising flour
500g (1lb) oats
500g (1lb) sugar
75g (3oz) sultanas
500g (1lb) butter
2 tbsp golden syrup
2 tbsp hot water
1 tsp bicarbonate of soda

Here's how
Preheat the oven to 180°C/350°F/Gas Mark 4. Line a baking tray with baking parchment.

Mix the flour, oats, sugar and sultanas together.

Melt the butter, syrup and water together in a pan over a low heat.

Add the bicarbonate of soda to the melted butter mixture, then stir in the flour mixture.

Mix together, then tip the mixture out on to a work surface. Press flat with your hands, or use a rolling pin and a little flour for dusting, until it is approx 1cm (½in) thick.

Using a round cutter, cut out the biscuits and place them on the baking tray. Bake for 15 minutes until golden.

Mars bar cakes

These are great to have on standby in an airtight container in the cupboard. They're one of those quick snacks every parent needs in their arsenal for when the kids are hungry. And making cakes using breakfast cereals is a classic starting point for getting kids in the kitchen.

INGREDIENTS

5 standard-size Mars bars

2 tbsp golden syrup

150g (5oz) butter

enough Rice Krispies to absorb the mixture – approx 100g (3½oz)

200g (7oz) white chocolate

Here's how

Grease an oblong tin – approx 15 x 30cm (6 x 12in) – and line with baking parchment.

Melt the Mars bars, syrup and butter in a small pan. When combined add the Rice Krispies and stir until coated.

Press the mixture into the lined tin and leave to set.

Melt the white chocolate in a bowl over a pan of simmering water. Don't be tempted to stir it, just let it melt gently, then pour it over the top of the cake. Cut into squares when cold and store in an airtight container.

British ale cake

This recipe is based on a traditional Irish recipe that uses porter, but I have replaced the beer with my local dark ale – Jennings Sneck Lifter. It's a great recipe that allows you to make it your own by using a beer brewed locally to you.

INGREDIENTS
175g (6oz) butter
175g (6oz) brown sugar
450g (14oz) mixed dried fruit
250ml (8fl oz) dark strong ale
½ tsp ground mixed spice
juice and zest of 1 orange
4 large eggs
1 tsp bicarbonate of soda
300g (10oz) plain flour
125g (4oz) walnuts
125g (4oz) hazelnuts

Here's how
Preheat the oven to 160°C/325°F/Gas Mark 3.

Put the butter, half the sugar, the dried fruit and beer in a large pan on a low heat. Add the mixed spice, orange zest and juice. I also throw the empty orange halves in while the mixture is cooking to give it a bit more flavour, but fish them out before you add the bicarb – see below.

Meanwhile use an electric whisk to mix the eggs and remaining sugar until the mixture has doubled in size and has become really light and fluffy.

When the pan ingredients have come to the boil, add the bicarbonate of soda and watch it fizz. Remove the pan from the heat: as the mixture cools it will catch all the air the bicarb has created. From this point onwards you need to work quickly to get the cake in the oven.

Pour in the egg mixture and sift in the plain flour. Add the nuts and mix it all together with a spoon and put into a 20 x 20cm (8 x 8in) cake tin and bake in the oven for 45 minutes.

Passion fruit curd

Passion fruit curd is my mum's favourite. Every time I go home to visit my parents I have to take her a jar. It's great on warm toast and I think it's amazing spooned on to a little vanilla ice cream or served up with some nice scones or bread muffins. So, Mum, here's the recipe – now I won't have to make it every time I come over.

INGREDIENTS

6 large egg yolks
100g (3½oz) caster sugar
juice and zest of ½ a lime
250g (8oz) butter
pulp from 6 passion fruits

Here's how

Whisk the egg yolks and sugar in a metal bowl for approx 1 minute.

Then add the lime zest and juice. Dice the butter and add to the bowl.

Place the bowl over a pan half full of just-boiling water and continue to whisk for 10 minutes.

Add the passion fruit pulp, including the seeds, and continue to whisk until all the butter has melted and the curd starts to thicken up.

To test whether the curd is ready, spoon a little on to a cold plate (keep the plate in the fridge until you're ready to use it). If the curd starts to set – if you can push your finger through it and it leaves an impression – then it is ready to transfer into clean sterilised jam jars. The curd will keep in the fridge for a couple of weeks.

Savoury muffins

When you say you are baking fresh muffins, people automatically think blueberry, lemon or chocolate. So, me being me, I thought why not take out the fruit and sugar and add a tasty mature Cheddar instead? Served with a piping hot bowl of soup, savoury muffins make a great alternative to bread rolls – or hand them round as nibbles at parties.

MAKES APPROX 9 MUFFINS

INGREDIENTS

300ml (½ pint) whole milk

2 large eggs

75ml (3fl oz) olive oil

150g (5oz) Cheddar, grated

75g (3oz) smoked cheese, grated

2 tbsp chopped fresh chives

salt and black pepper

450g (14oz) plain flour

3 tsp baking powder

Here's how

Preheat the oven to 160°C/325°F/Gas Mark 3.

Whisk together the milk, eggs and oil. Add the grated cheeses and chopped chives and season with a little salt and pepper.

Sift the flour and baking powder into the bowl and carefully fold into the mixture.

Cut some baking parchment into 10cm (4in) squares and use them to line the wells in a muffin tin – or use muffin cases instead.

Divide the mixture equally between the wells or muffin cases and bake for 25 minutes until golden and cooked.

Savoury walnut shortbread

These savoury shortbreads are the ultimate addition to any cheese board. Once you've tried them your usual box of biscuits for cheese will stay in the cupboard. They are so easy to make: the dough will keep in the fridge for a few weeks – or you can slice it into biscuits and freeze them until you're ready to bake.

INGREDIENTS

250g (8oz) butter

125g (4oz) Parmesan, grated

pinch of cayenne pepper

salt

1 large egg yolk

100g (3½oz) toasted walnuts

325g (11oz) plain flour

Here's how

Put the butter and grated Parmesan in a bowl, add the cayenne pepper and a sprinkle of salt, followed by the egg yolk, and beat together until light and fluffy.

Add the walnuts and the flour. Mix together until it forms a crumbly texture.

Transfer the contents of the bowl to a work surface. Use your hands to mould it together into a long triangular log. Wrap in clingfilm and leave in the fridge for an hour.

Preheat the oven to 160°C/325°F/Gas Mark 3. Cut the log into 1–2cm (½–¾in) slices. Place them on a non-stick baking tray and bake for approximately 12 minutes – they should be lovely and golden.

Bourbon biscuits

These biscuits are among my all-time favourites. I have great childhood memories of raiding the family cookie jar when my parents weren't looking, and hiding out somewhere to enjoy them. They are surprisingly easy to make and taste fantastic – a real trip down memory lane.

MAKES APPROX 12 BISCUITS

INGREDIENTS

250g (8oz) butter

250g (8oz) caster sugar

1 egg

1 tsp vanilla essence

375g (12oz) plain flour

1 tbsp cocoa powder

1½ tsp baking powder

For the butter-cream filling

125g (4oz) icing sugar, sifted

2 tbsp butter, softened

½ tsp vanilla essence

1 tbsp cocoa powder

Here's how

Cream the butter and caster sugar until light and fluffy. Gradually beat in the egg and vanilla essence.

Sift the dry ingredients and fold into mixture to make a dough. Put the dough in the fridge and leave to chill for 30 minutes – this makes it easier to roll out.

Preheat the oven to 180–190°C/350–375°F/Gas Mark 4–5.

Divide the dough in half and roll out each half out to approximately 0.5cm (¼in) thick. Cut the dough into rectangles approx x 8cm (¾ x 3in).

Line a baking tray with baking parchment. Lay the rectangles on the tray, leaving about 2.5cm (1in) between each, and make a few holes in the top of each biscuit with a fork. Bake for 15 minutes, then cool on a wire rack.

Meanwhile make the butter-cream. Gradually beat half the icing sugar into the softened butter, then add the vanilla essence. Add the remaining icing sugar and cocoa powder.

When the biscuits are cool, join pairs together with butter-cream. Store in an airtight container.

Tip

If you're stuck for a quick dessert, crush a few of the biscuits over some vanilla ice cream.

Custard creams

These biscuits are another blast from the past – I'd forgotten how much I enjoy them. Making them at home is a lot of fun and I think they taste better than the shop-bought ones. The question is, how do you eat yours? Do you just tuck in or are you one of those people who bite open the biscuit and lick the icing?

MAKES APPROX 12 BISCUITS

INGREDIENTS
250g (8oz) butter
250g (8oz) caster sugar
1 egg
1 tsp vanilla essence
325g (11oz) plain flour
75g (3oz) custard powder
1½ tsp baking powder

For the butter-cream filling
125g (4oz) icing sugar, sifted
2 tbsp butter, softened
½ tsp vanilla essence
2 tbsp condensed milk

Here's how
Preheat the oven to 180–190°C/350–375°F/Gas Mark 4–5.

Cream the butter and caster sugar until light and fluffy. Gradually beat in the egg and vanilla essence.

Sift the dry ingredients and fold into the mixture to form a dough. Break off pieces of dough and roll them into small balls.

Place them on an ungreased baking tray and press down with a fork to flatten. Then bake for 15 minutes. Cool the biscuits on a wire rack.

Meanwhile make the butter-cream filling. Gradually beat half the icing sugar into the softened butter, then add the vanilla essence. Beat in the condensed milk and add the remaining icing sugar.

When the biscuits have cooled, join pairs together with butter-cream.

Tip
For a quick and easy tiramisu, soak the biscuits in a little espresso coffee, top with sweetened mascarpone and dust with cocoa powder.

Rainy days

Get up and go flapjacks

As well as being a tea-time treat, these flapjacks are great for breakfast on the go. Shove one in your teenager's hand as he or she heads for the door. I've added some coffee to the recipe, just to give everyone a little bit extra get up and go in the morning.

MAKES APPROX 12 BARS

INGREDIENTS
a handful each of hazelnuts and
    walnuts
300g (10oz) butter
4 tbsp golden syrup
340g (11½oz) caster sugar
200ml (7fl oz) condensed milk
450g (14oz) porridge oats
2 tbsp good-quality instant coffee
50g (2oz) chopped dates

Here's how
Preheat the oven to 160°C/325°F/Gas Mark 3.

Put the nuts on a baking tray and toast for 10 minutes until golden.

Line a baking tray (approx 22 x 23cm/9 x 9in) with baking parchment.

Melt the butter, syrup and sugar in a large pan over a low heat. When they have melted, add the condensed milk and remove from the heat. Add the oats and coffee, then mix together.

Stir in the toasted nuts and chopped dates and spoon the mixture into the lined tin and bake for 15–20 minutes.

Remove from the oven and leave to cool for 30 minutes.

While the flapjack is still warm, cut it into 16 portions. Store in an airtight container when cool.

Caramel dodgers

Forget jammy dodgers, my caramel versions are something else. The best method I know of making caramel is to boil up a can of condensed milk, but just don't let the pan boil dry! It produces the richest, sweetest, best-tasting caramel there is.

MAKES APPROX 12 BISCUITS

INGREDIENTS
250g (8oz) butter
250g (8oz) caster sugar
1 egg
1 tsp vanilla essence
325g (11oz) plain flour
75g (3oz) custard powder
1½ tsp baking powder

For the filling
1 can condensed milk

Here's how

Start by making the caramel filling. Put the can of condensed milk in a saucepan of water and boil for 2½ hours, making sure you top up the water as necessary. Leave the can to cool for at least an hour before opening.

Preheat the oven to 180–190°C/350–375°F/Gas Mark 4–5.

Cream the butter and caster sugar until light and fluffy. Gradually beat in the egg and vanilla essence.

Sift the dry ingredients and fold into the mixture to form a dough.

Roll out the dough to around 0.5cm (¼in) thick and use a fluted cutter to stamp out the biscuits. Cut a small hole in the middle of half of the biscuits.

Put the biscuits on an ungreased baking tray and bake for 15 minutes.

When the biscuits have cooled, join them in pairs with the caramel.

Comfort food

When it's cold outside, there's nothing better than coming home and walking through the door to be hit by the wonderful aroma of a slow-cooked stew that you know will really warm you up. Comfort food is one of my favourite types of cooking; for me, it symbolises cooking from the heart. In this chapter I have included a real mixture of different dishes, from my famous sausage rolls to a wonderful version of melanzane, my favourite Italian vegetarian dish.

Quick jacket potatoes

A great mixture of baked potato, strong Cheddar and Worcestershire sauce – the perfect combination of melted cheese and crispy potato skin. To turn this into a complete meal, grill some dry cured bacon and add a dressed crisp salad. Delicious.

INGREDIENTS

4 large jacket potatoes

oil, for rubbing

salt and black pepper

50g (2oz) butter

75g (3oz) mature Cheddar, grated

3–4 tsp Worcestershire sauce

Here's how

Preheat the oven to 200°C/400°F/Gas Mark 6.

Cook the potatoes in the microwave for about 6 minutes at 750 watt setting.

To crisp up the skins, rub the cooked potatoes all over with some oil and salt. Transfer to a baking sheet and blast them in the oven for 15 minutes.

When the potatoes are cooked, carefully cut them in half to allow them to cool and release all the steam. Once they have cooled a little, using a metal spoon scoop out the white fluffy potato into a mixing bowl and season with a little salt and pepper.

Add the butter and half the cheese, then beat with a wooden spoon or mash with a potato masher until smooth.

Scoop the mashed potato back into the hollow skins and top with the remaining cheese, add a few dashes of Worcestershire sauce and put them back in the oven at 180˚C/350˚F/Gas Mark 4 until golden and bubbly – about 10 minutes.

Tip

Cooking potatoes in the microwave then finishing them off in the conventional oven means you don't miss out on crispy skin.

Sausage rolls with fennel and apple chutney

Homemade sausage rolls are delicious – we've forgotten just how great they are. I showed viewers how I make mine on my first TV series, and from that day on people stop me in the street to tell me how wonderful they are. I'll say no more – just get in the kitchen and knock up a batch for yourself and you'll see what I'm talking about.

INGREDIENTS

250g (8oz) packet puff pastry

500g (1lb) Cumberland sausages

1 large egg, lightly whisked

1 tsp fennel seeds (optional)

For the chutney

2 fennel bulbs, roughly chopped

1 onion, roughly chopped

olive oil, for drizzling

1 apple, roughly chopped

100ml (3½fl oz) white wine vinegar

350g (11oz) preserving sugar

1 tsp fennel seeds

salt and black pepper

Here's how

Make the chutney. Put the fennel and onion in a heavy pan. Add a drizzle of olive oil and cook until soft, then add the roughly chopped apple and cook for a few more minutes.

Add the white wine vinegar, sugar and fennel seeds. Continue to cook for a further 20 minutes until the liquid has reduced by half. Season with salt and pepper and leave to cool.

Preheat the oven to 180°C/350°F/Gas Mark 4.

Cut the block of puff pastry in half. Roll each half into a long rectangle, about 40 x 10cm (16 x 4in) and about 0.5cm (¼in) thick. Spread a tablespoon of fennel chutney down the middle of each rectangle. (Store the rest of the chutney in clean sterilised jars – it will keep for around 4 weeks in the fridge.)

Cut the sausagemeat out of the skins and lay it on top of the chutney. Pull the pastry over the sausagemeat and press the edges together.

Cut each long sausage roll into approx 10 portions. Place the rolls on a non-stick baking tray and brush them with the beaten egg. Sprinkle with fennel seeds if using and bake for 15 minutes until golden brown.

French onion tart

This rich sweet onion tart is amazing straight out of the oven. I am told it's lovely cold too, but I don't think I will ever find out for myself as I can never wait for it to cool down. Serve it for lunch with a toasted walnut and rocket salad, dressed in a little olive oil and sherry vinegar.

INGREDIENTS

For the pastry

300g (10oz) plain flour

150g (5oz) butter

pinch of salt

(or use a 300g/10oz packet of readymade shortcrust pastry)

For the filling

25g (1oz) butter

2 tbsp olive oil

1kg (2lb) onions, halved then thinly sliced

salt and black pepper

1 tbsp chopped thyme

1 garlic clove, crushed then chopped

2 medium eggs

150ml (¼ pint) double cream

150ml (¼ pint) milk

50g (2oz) Emmental cheese, grated

40g (1½oz) Parmesan, grated

Here's how

Preheat the oven to 190°C/375°F/Gas Mark 5.

Make the pastry. Put the flour and butter into a food processor and blend to a crumb, then add the pinch of salt and 4 tbsp cold water, turn the mixer back on using a pulse setting until you have a pastry dough. Cover the dough in clingfilm and rest in the fridge for 10 minutes.

Roll out the pastry on a lightly floured surface and use to line a deep 23cm (9in) fluted flan tin. Line the pastry with baking parchment and fill with baking beans. Bake blind for 15 minutes.

Heat the butter and oil in a large frying pan, then gently fry the onions. Cook the onions for about 30 minutes until completely softened. Season them with plenty of salt and pepper as this will help you achieve that lovely golden caramel colour.

Add the chopped thyme and garlic about 15 minutes before the end.

Beat the eggs, cream and milk together in a bowl, then add the cheeses and some seasoning. Stir in the onions, then spoon the mixture into the flan case. Bake for 25–30 minutes until lightly set and browned.

Belly pork with cider, apple and black pudding

Whenever I roast belly pork, I always buy a bigger joint than I actually need for one reason and one reason only – so I can make this dish the next day. I love the combination of crispy pork, black pudding and sweet apple all cooked in cider. It just makes perfect sense on a plate.

INGREDIENTS

1.5kg (3lb) belly pork

salt and black pepper

2 onions, cut into eighths

2 tbsp olive oil

1 tsp fennel seeds

6 slices (approx 250g/8oz total weight) of black pudding

4 apples, peeled and cut into quarters

6–8 sage leaves

few sprigs of rosemary

500ml (17fl oz) cider

Here's how

Preheat the oven to 220˚C/425˚F/Gas Mark 7.

Cut the belly pork into pieces and rub the skin of each piece with seasoning. Scatter the onions in a shallow roasting tin and pour over 1 tbsp of the olive oil. Season. Lay the pork on top, sprinkle the skin with fennel seeds and put in the oven for 30 minutes to start off the crackling.

Add the slices of black pudding, apple, sage leaves and rosemary after the 30 minutes are up. Pour the cider around the pork and turn the oven down to 180˚C/350˚F/Gas Mark 4. Cook for a further 40 minutes or until the pork is tender.

If using leftover pork

If using leftovers from the recipe for BBQ Pork (page 79), cut the meat into chunks about 3–4cm (1¼–1½in) thick so that they won't dry out.

Cut the black pudding into similar sized chunks. Place them in an ovenproof dish with the quartered apples and the onions.

Add the cider, seasoning, sage leaves and rosemary to the dish.

Cover with foil and bake in a preheated oven at 180˚C/350˚F/Gas Mark 4. Remove the foil after 30 minutes to let things crisp up and cook for a further 30 minutes.

Lamb hash with poached eggs

If you don't usually have much lamb left over after a roast dinner, you might not want to tell anyone else you are making this dish – otherwise they'll all want some. A softly poached egg is the perfect accompaniment to this real comfort food.

INGREDIENTS

1 large potato

200g (7oz) or so left-over cooked lamb

200g (7oz) haggis

3 spring onions

4 eggs plus 1 extra yolk

chopped flat-leaf parsley, to serve

black pepper, to serve

For the salsa

handful of mint

handful of flat-leaf parsley

1 garlic clove

2 tbsp capers

1 tsp Dijon mustard

4 tbsp white wine vinegar

4 tbsp extra-virgin olive oil

salt and black pepper

Here's how

Wash the potato and pierce it with a fork repeatedly, then cook it in the microwave until soft all the way through – about 6 minutes at 750 watt setting. When it is cooked carefully cut it in half to let out all the steam. The reason I make mashed potato this way is that it keeps its flavour really well: letting out the steam concentrates the flavour while getting rid of excess water.

Chop the cooked lamb as finely as possible and place in a bowl. Break up the haggis and add to the lamb. Chop the spring onions and add them too.

When the potato has cooled a little, scoop it out and add to the lamb mixture.

Scrunch it all up to mix all the flavours together.

Add the egg yolk and mix again – you are aiming for a fish-cake-type texture.

Divide the mixture into portions. Wet hands make it a lot easier to shape the cakes. I like to make one good-sized one per person, but you can make smaller ones if you wish, or even one big one to share.

Make the salsa. Put all the ingredients into a food processor and blend until smooth. Season with a little salt and pepper if required.

Brush the cakes with a little oil and fry in a non-stick frying pan for 3–4 minutes on each side until golden. Keep them warm in the oven while you poach the eggs (see page 163 for the best way to do this).

Serve each cake topped with a poached egg. Add a drizzle of salsa, scatter with flat-leaf parsley and finish with a few twists of pepper.

Boar burger with gingerbread

After a long lunch with the owners of the world famous Grasmere Gingerbread Shop in the Lake District (see page 90), they challenged me to come up with a dish using the crumbs left over from their baking process – something other than a cheesecake base. I've been making these burgers for years now. Ginger and coriander taste great together.

INGREDIENTS

1kg (2lb) wild boar sausages, skinned

150g (5oz) Grasmere gingerbread, crumbled, or use ordinary ginger biscuits with an extra tsp of ground ginger

2 tbsp coriander seeds

handful of fresh coriander

salt and black pepper

oil, for frying

4 bread rolls

bag of mixed salad leaves

salad dressing of your choice

4 tbsp chilli jam

lime wedges, to serve

Here's how

Put the boar sausagemeat in a bowl. Add the gingerbread/biscuit crumbs and mix well.

Put the whole coriander seeds into a dry frying pan and heat until they start to crackle – this will really bring out the perfume of the seeds and increase the flavour. Chop the fresh coriander stalks finely and add to the mixture – save the leaves to go in the bread rolls. Mix well using your hands. Season with salt and pepper.

Shape into burgers and store in the fridge until needed.

Heat a little oil in a frying pan. Add the burgers and cook for 5 minutes on each side until firm. Or cook them in the oven for 15–20 minutes at 180°C/350°F/Gas Mark 4.

Serve the burgers in bread rolls with dressed salad leaves, a tbsp of chilli jam each, the fresh coriander leaves and finally a squeeze of lime to bring it all to life.

Toad in the hole

Toad in the hole is a traditional and popular family dish. People ask me all the time how I make mine. Well, being an 'adopted' Yorkshire man who now lives in Cumbria, here's my method. It is really important that you don't weigh out the ingredients for Yorkshire pudding – it's all about using equal volumes. Use a cup or a mug – it must be the same one – to measure the eggs, milk and flour. I use a 200ml (7fl oz) coffee cup.

INGREDIENTS

1 cup of plain flour

1 cup of eggs, beaten

1 cup of milk

8 good-quality sausages (Cumberland are my favourite)

3 red onions, cut into chunks

sprig of rosemary, leaves chopped

sprig of thyme, leaves chopped

4 tbsp olive oil

salt and black pepper

Here's how

Measure out the flour, eggs and milk using the same-sized cup for all three. It is important to use equal quantities by volume of each.

Whisk them together to form a smooth lump-free batter. The best way to do this is to make a well in the centre of the flour and pour the eggs in. Then start whisking the eggs, gradually incorporating the flour. Finally, whisk in the milk a little at a time. Leave the batter to rest for at least 1 hour.

Preheat the oven to 200˚C/400˚F/Gas Mark 6.

Put the sausages in a roasting tray with deep sides and space them apart. Scatter the onions and herbs on top and drizzle with oil. Season with a little salt and pepper and bake for 15–20 minutes until the sausages are starting to colour and the onion is tinged brown at the edges.

Remove the tray from the oven and quickly pour the batter over the sausages. Return to the oven for a further 35–40 minutes until the batter is crisp and well risen.

Fish and chips with a twist

Homemade fish and chips is a great British classic, but not many people have a deep-fat fryer these days as it stinks the house out and, let's be honest, it's not the healthiest way of cooking. But don't be put off cooking your own fish and chips. This recipe will make you want to wrap your dinner up in newspaper and stand outside to eat it.

INGREDIENTS

8 slices of bread

handful of flat-leaf parsley

1 tbsp fresh tarragon

4 fresh mackerel, gutted and
    heads removed

2 medium celeriac

4 tbsp olive oil

salt and black pepper

1 tbsp fennel seeds

1 lemon, cut into wedges, to serve

Here's how

Preheat the oven to 180°C/350°F/Gas Mark 4.

Put the bread and herbs in a food processor and blend to fine crumbs.

Prepare the fish. Make two cuts down the middle of the fish, on either side of the backbone, at about a 45° angle, then lift out the strip of bones.

Peel the celeriac and cut them into chips. Put the chips in a bowl with the olive oil and stir them around so they all get a coating of oil – this will ensure they crisp up in the oven.

Season with salt, pepper and fennel seeds.

Tip the chips onto a non-stick baking tray and bake for 25 minutes, until soft in the middle and crispy on the outside.

Meanwhile place the fish fillets skin-side down on a baking tray lined with a piece of lightly oiled baking parchment.

Season with a little salt and pepper, then top with the breadcrumbs. Using your hand just pat the crumbs down – add a few more if you can still see any fish.

Bake the fish for 15 minutes alongside the chips so that they are ready at the same time. The breadcrumbs should go golden and crispy. Serve with lemon wedges.

Melanzane

Melanzane is one of my favourite vegetarian dishes. My version has been tested on Italians – it got my friend Francesco's nod of approval when I cooked it on holiday in Tuscany, so it must be OK. Not many Italians approve anything unless it's made the way their mother does it.

INGREDIENTS

1 medium-sized onion

3 garlic cloves

1 x 400g can chopped tomatoes

1 vegetable stock cube

4 medium-sized aubergines

olive oil, for drizzling

salt and black pepper

2 x 125g (4oz) mozzarella balls

1 basil plant or approx 20–25 leaves

4 slices of bread

2 sprigs of rosemary, leaves only

100g (3½oz) Parmesan, grated

Here's how

Preheat the oven to 160°C/325°F/Gas Mark 3.

Peel and finely chop the onion and garlic and put them in a medium-sized saucepan with the chopped tomatoes, 200ml (7fl oz) water and the stock cube. Place the pan over a medium heat and bring to the boil, then turn the heat down and leave to simmer for 30 minutes.

Meanwhile cut the top and bottom off the aubergines and then carefully slice them lengthwise to create wide strips like lasagne sheets.

Drizzle some olive oil over a large baking tray, then sprinkle it with salt and pepper. Lay the slices of aubergine on top of the oil and seasoning and then turn them over so that both sides are coated.

Cook the aubergine slices in the oven for 15–20 minutes: they don't need to be completely cooked, just supple enough to roll around the mozzarella. Leave to cool.

Slice each ball of mozzarella into 8 pieces and lay them on a chopping board. Put one basil leaf on top of each slice of mozzarella.

When the aubergines have cooled down a little, wrap a slice of aubergine around each slice of mozzarella so that it encases it like a jacket, then arrange them in an ovenproof dish.

Taste the tomato sauce and season with salt and pepper if required. Chop the remaining basil and add to the sauce, then spoon the sauce over the aubergines to cover them.

Turn the oven up to 180°C/350°F/Gas Mark 4.

Put the bread in a food processor with the rosemary leaves and grated Parmesan and blend together until the rosemary has been chopped up.

Sprinkle the breadcrumbs over the aubergines and finish with a final drizzle of olive oil to help them crisp up in the oven. Bake for 30–40 minutes.

Pork chops with roasted pears and star anise

Pork and fruit are great partners and this dish is a real celebration of seasonal British autumn produce. September through to November are great months for the kitchen as they offer so many delicious opportunities.

INGREDIENTS

4 pears

3 red onions

large sprig of rosemary

sprig of thyme

3–4 whole star anise

olive oil, for drizzling

salt and black pepper

4 pork chops, around 200g (7oz) each

Here's how

Preheat the oven to 180°C/350°F/Gas Mark 4.

Peel and quarter the pears and red onions.

Put them in a cast-iron roasting dish with the chopped rosemary, thyme and star anise. Drizzle with a little olive oil, season with salt and pepper and roast in the oven for 25 minutes.

Put a non-stick frying pan on to heat. Season the pork chops with salt, pepper and a drizzle of olive oil.

When the frying pan is hot, add the chops and cook for 1–2 minutes on each side until golden brown. When the chops are a lovely nutty colour on each side, transfer to the roasting dish with the pears to finish cooking – give them another 10–15 minutes.

Comfort food

Blackberry Bakewell

Bakewell tart is one of my wife's favourites and a bit of a British classic. It makes perfect sense to add blackberries in season if you've been out picking. At other times of year, use blackberry and apple jam instead. Serve up the tart with lots of vanilla ice cream.

INGREDIENTS

For the pastry

300g (10oz) plain flour, plus extra for dusting

125g (4oz) unsalted butter

25g (1oz) sugar

1 free-range egg, plus 1 extra, beaten, to glaze

2 tbsp milk, to bind (if needed)

For the filling

250g (8oz) butter, softened

250g (8oz) sugar

250g (8oz) ground almonds

3 free-range eggs

finely grated zest of 1 lemon

50g (2oz) plain flour

200g (7oz) fresh blackberries, crushed with a fork or 1 jar of apple and blackberry jam

flaked almonds, for sprinkling

icing sugar, for dusting

Here's how

For the pastry, put the flour, butter, sugar and egg in a food processor and pulse to combine. If necessary, add a little milk to help bring the mixture together.

Turn the dough out on to a floured work surface and roll it out until large enough to line a 25cm (10in) tart tin. Carefully lift the pastry into the tin, then chill in the fridge for an hour.

Preheat the oven to 200°C/400°F/Gas Mark 6.

Line the tart case with a sheet of greaseproof paper and fill with baking beans or rice. Bake the tart case blind in the oven for 15–20 minutes.

Remove the paper and beans and brush the pastry all over with the beaten egg. Return to the oven for a further 5 minutes, until golden-brown. Remove from the oven and turn the oven down to 180°C/350°F/Gas Mark 4.

For the filling, beat the butter and sugar together in a bowl until pale and fluffy. Mix in the ground almonds, then crack in the eggs one at a time, beating well between each addition – don't worry if the mixture begins to split, just add a little of the flour. Fold in the lemon zest and the flour.

Spread the crushed blackberries generously across the base of the tart case, leaving a 2.5cm (1in) gap around the edge or spread with jam.

Spread the filling mixture over the berries or jam and sprinkle with the flaked almonds.

Transfer to the oven and bake for 20 minutes, or until set and golden-brown. Allow to cool in the tin before dusting with icing sugar and serving.

Days out

We all know food tastes better outdoors. Instead of packing up sandwiches for an outing, why not be a bit more adventurous and take a portable barbecue? These recipes are great for everything from a picnic on the beach to a hike across the fields. And there's nothing to stop you cooking them at home in the garden too. The other angle I've emphasised here is recipes to make when you get back from a day out fruit picking or fishing. Ever since my daughter was tall enough we've taken her raspberry picking, so I've included my recipes for raspberry jam, pink lemonade and raspberry muffins. And I'm a keen fisherman and love nothing more than cooking my catch right there on the bank.

Pink lemonade

Pink lemonade is that little bit different and something new to try with those raspberries you've just picked. It's so easy to make. I like to freeze a plastic bottleful to make fresh summery drinks in winter, but you can make it out of season using frozen raspberries instead.

INGREDIENTS

zest and juice of 1½ lemons

300g (10oz) caster sugar

150g (5oz) raspberries, fresh or frozen

Here's how

Put the lemon zest, juice and sugar in a pan over a medium heat and stir until the sugar dissolves.

Add the raspberries and 350ml (12fl oz) cold water, bring the mixture to the boil, then turn off the heat and leave to cool.

Pour the cooled syrup through a sieve, pressing the raspberries through the sieve.

You can store the syrup in the fridge for up to 1 week.

To serve, pour a little into a glass and top up with sparkling or still water.

Tip

To make funky ice cubes to serve with the drinks, add individual fresh raspberries to the compartments in your ice-cube tray and freeze.

Trout with ham, lemon and rosemary

I love fly fishing and just wish I could go more often and cook what I catch. When I do get the chance and actually hook a few trout, this is how I cook them. If you're confident of reeling in a few, take a portable barbecue along and cook them at the water's edge.

INGREDIENTS

3–4 whole trout, depending on
  size, gutted

1 lemon

75g (3oz) butter

4 sprigs of rosemary

salt and black pepper

6–8 slices of cured ham, such as
  serrano or Parma

olive oil, for brushing or drizzling

Here's how

Get the barbecue going. Or if you're cooking your catch back home, preheat the oven to 180°C/350°F/Gas Mark 4.

Make 4 cuts 1cm (½in) deep in each side of the fish, to allow flavours in.

Slice the lemon thinly and cut the butter into small cubes. Divide the lemon slices and butter between the fish, putting them inside the belly cavity along with a sprig of rosemary and plenty of seasoning.

Wrap the fish in the slices of ham to encase all the flavours.

Cook the fish directly on the barbecue grill. Just brush a little oil straight on to the ham and fish so it does not stick. Put them on a cool part of the barbecue: don't put them in the middle where it is smoking hot. Cook for 10 minutes on each side or until cooked right through.

If cooking the fish at home, lay them on a non-stick baking tray with a drizzle of olive oil and cook in the oven for 25 minutes.

Roasted mushrooms

This is a great way to cook mushrooms on the barbecue. Cooking them in foil makes sure all the flavours stay in with the mushrooms and stops them drying out. Or just put them in the oven – they taste fantastic either way.

INGREDIENTS

1 garlic bulb

500g (1lb) chestnut mushrooms

2 tbsp olive oil

50g (2oz) butter

2 tbsp chopped thyme

2 tbsp chopped rosemary

sea salt and black pepper

Here's how

Separate the garlic cloves and lightly crush each one with the flat of a knife. Put the cloves in the centre of a 40cm (16in) square piece of foil.

Slice the mushrooms in half and pile them on top of the garlic.

Drizzle over the olive oil and lay the slab of butter on top. Sprinkle with the chopped herbs and season with sea salt and pepper.

Scrunch up the foil to encase the mushrooms.

Cook the parcel on the barbecue for 20 minutes or bung it in the oven at 180°C/350°F/Gas Mark 4 for 30 minutes, until all the mushrooms are cooked and the rest of the ingredients have melted together to make an amazing sauce.

Serve up the mushrooms with chunks of bread to catch all the garlic sauce.

Raspberry jam

As a family we enjoy finding pick-your-own farms that grow fantastic soft fruits – it's one of our favourite days out. After eating our fill of fresh fruit, I like to make raspberry jam. There's no better reminder of summer than a spoonful of fresh-tasting raspberry jam on your toast.

INGREDIENTS
625g (1¼lb) preserving sugar
500g (1lb) raspberries
zest and juice of 1 lime

Here's how
Put the sugar, raspberries and lime zest into a heavy-based pan. Using a wooden spoon, mix the sugar and raspberries together – this is an important step: it makes the jam taste really fresh.

Cook on a medium heat until the jam boils, then continue to cook for approximately 5 minutes more. If the jam starts to boil rapidly, stand a large metal spoon in the pan and reduce the heat – this should slow things down.

Once the jam has boiled for 5 minutes, add the lime juice and mix together.

Leave the jam to cool for about 20–30 minutes, then pour it into clean sterilised jam jars.

The jam should keep in the fridge for about 3 months, but if your household is anything like mine, it won't last that long.

Kids' mango and raspberry parcels

When you've been fruit picking, it's nice to be able to show the kids how to cook with fruit rather than just eat it out of the punnet. Make some jam (see page 144), then try these parcels. Kids love making and eating them. You'll have to buy the mango, of course – make sure it's ripe.

INGREDIENTS

200g (7oz) plain yogurt, any sort

2 tbsp olive oil

250g (8oz) self-raising flour

salt and black pepper

4 tbsp raspberry jam
(see recipe on page 144)

1 fresh mango, peeled and
chopped into cubes, about
1cm (½ in)

1 lime

Here's how

Preheat the oven to 180°C/350°F/Gas Mark 4.

Mix the yogurt and oil together in a bowl. Add the flour and a little salt and pepper, and mix to form a smooth dough – but try not to over-mix it. Transfer the dough to a floured work surface and divide into 12 portions.

Mix the raspberry jam with the cubed mango.

Roll out each portion of dough into a circle approximately 0.25cm thick.

Place a spoonful of the jam mixture along the middle of each circle and top with a squeeze of lime. Brush the edges with a little water. Fold over two sides of the circle, then roll up to form something that looks like a spring roll.

Place on a non-stick baking tray and bake for 15 minutes until golden and crisp. Be very careful as the filling will be extremely hot.

Raspberry and lime muffins

My muffins had quite a following in my deli. We would make about 100 a day and they were all gone just after lunch. Now you can try them at home for yourselves. This is a great recipe for using up any seasonal fruit at any time of the year. The uncooked batter will keep for a couple of weeks in the fridge or you can bake a batch and freeze them just as easily.

INGREDIENTS

2 eggs

225g (7½oz) granulated sugar

500ml (17fl oz) milk

1 tsp vanilla extract

125ml (4fl oz) sunflower oil

375g (12oz) plain flour

3 tsp bicarbonate of soda

½ tsp salt

100g (3½oz) oats

250g (8oz) raspberries, fresh or frozen

zest of 1 lime

Here's how

Whisk the eggs and sugar together in a bowl, then pour in the milk and vanilla extract. Stir well, then add the sunflower oil.

Sift the flour with the bicarbonate of soda and salt, and fold into the egg mixture. Add the oats, mix again and cover tightly until needed.

Preheat the oven to 180°C/350°F/Gas Mark 4.

Stir the mixture before using, then add the raspberries and lime zest and mix together.

Stand muffin cases in a muffin tin and fill them three quarters full. Bake for 15–20 minutes, or until firm to the touch and golden. Cool the muffins on a wire rack before serving.

BBQ peaches

People always ask me what to do for dessert when they are having a barbecue. I say make the most of the hot grill by chucking on a few peaches – summer is their proper season. Serve them up with some good-quality vanilla ice cream.

INGREDIENTS

8 peaches

3 tbsp olive oil

1 tsp chopped fresh rosemary

2 tbsp runny honey

juice of 1 lemon

Here's how

Cut the peaches in half, remove the stones and arrange the fruit on a baking tray cut-side up. Drizzle with the olive oil, then cook them on a medium heat on the barbecue. If cooking at home, put them under a preheated grill or use a preheated griddle pan.

Don't cook the peaches for too long: do it just enough to get that lovely charred, caramelised flavour – about 5–6 minutes should be fine.

While the peaches are cooking mix the rosemary, honey and lemon juice together. Pour the dressing over the warm peaches.

Feta and black olive parcels

I've borrowed the style of this pastry from *empanadas*, a great South American dish. It is strong and crisp so it can encase all kinds of different fillings – whatever takes your fancy. Get the kids to prepare their own parcels at home, then take them with you on a picnic to cook on a portable barbecue. Or cook them at home and eat them cold.

INGREDIENTS

200g (7oz) plain yogurt, any sort

2 tbsp olive oil

250g (8oz) self-raising flour

salt and black pepper

100g (3½oz) feta

16 kalamata olives

1 tsp dried mint

squeeze of lemon juice

Greek yogurt, to serve

lemon wedges, to serve

Here's how

Get the barbecue going or preheat the oven to 180°C/350°F/Gas Mark 4 if you're cooking in the kitchen.

Mix the yogurt and oil together in a bowl. Add the flour and a little salt and pepper, and mix together to form a smooth dough – try not to over mix it.

Crumble the feta cheese in a separate bowl and stir in the dried mint. Break the olives in half, add to the feta cheese and mix together.

Transfer the dough to a lightly floured work surface and divide into 12 portions. Roll out each portion of dough into a circle. Make them as thin as you possibly can – approximately 0.25cm is ideal.

Place a spoonful of the cheese mixture in the middle of each circle of dough and top with a squeeze of lemon juice and a twist of black pepper

Brush the edges of the pastry with a little water then fold over the parcel to make a semi-circle and crimp the edges shut to create a seal.

Cook the parcels directly on the barbecue grill for 15 minutes until golden and crisp. Or put the parcels on a non-stick baking tray and bake in the oven or cook them on a preheated grill pan.

Serve with Greek yogurt and lemon wedges.

Pork chops with BBQ peaches

We usually partner apple with pork in the UK, but the last time I was cooking some delicious pork chops on the barbecue I also had a handful of irresistibly tasty peaches. I put them on the barbecue while the pork cooked and they just sang together. You get a lovely sweet stickiness when you cook peaches that works so well with the pork.

INGREDIENTS

4 peaches, halved and stones removed

3 tbsp olive oil

knob of butter

4 large pork chops, about 200g (7oz) each

salt and black pepper

few sprigs of thyme

a wine glass full of dry cider

juice of ½ lemon

1 tbsp honey

Here's how

Get the barbecue going (or preheat the oven to 180°C/350°F/Gas Mark 4).

Drizzle the peaches with 2 tbsp of the olive oil and cook on the barbecue or roast them in the oven.

Meanwhile melt the butter. Use it to brush the chops, season them with salt and pepper then cook the chops on the barbecue grill for about 15 minutes, turning halfway through. If cooking at home, melt the butter over a moderate heat in a pan just large enough to take the chops. Add the chops, seasoning them with salt and black pepper and fry on both sides for a few minutes till the meat and fat are pale gold.

If you've grilled the chops on the barbecue, transfer them to a pan to finish cooking. In either case, add the thyme and cider to the pan. Cover and leave to cook on for 15 minutes or so.

Mix together the lemon juice, honey and remaining tbsp of olive oil, then pour over the cooked peaches and serve with the pork chops.

Blackberry crumble pots

These are a great way to enjoy a very seasonal British food that's there for the picking in the hedgerow. If you make the crumble in advance it will keep nice and crispy for weeks in an airtight container. This recipe can work as a simple last-minute dessert – or try it for breakfast.

INGREDIENTS
200g (7oz) blackberries
50g (2oz) sugar
10 fresh mint leaves, chopped
juice and zest of 1 lime
500g tub Greek yogurt

For the crumble
300g (10oz) flour
200g (7oz) butter
175g (6oz) sugar
zest of 1 lemon

Here's how
Preheat the oven to 160°C/325°F/Gas Mark 3.

To make the crumble, put the flour and butter into a mixing bowl. Using your finger tips, rub the butter into the flour to make a crumble texture. Add the sugar and lemon zest, then mix together.

Spread out the crumble mixture on a non-stick baking tray and bake for 15–20 minutes until golden and crumbly.

Leave to cool, then store in an airtight container until needed.

Put the blackberries in a mixing bowl with the sugar, chopped mint, lime juice and zest. Mix together and break up the berries a little with a fork.

Spoon half of the berries into 4 bowls or glasses. Add a layer of thick creamy Greek yogurt then the remaining blackberries. Finally top with the crumble and serve.

Fresh from the garden

Growing your own food is quite trendy these days. So if you have a bit of a veg plot in the garden, this chapter is for you. There really is nothing nicer than being able to eat what you grow – though of course these recipes will taste just as great if you've been shopping for top-quality British seasonal ingredients too. I have great memories of Sunday lunch at my in-laws'. When we arrived my father-in-law would be out in the garden digging up the potatoes – let me tell you, they were the best new potatoes I have ever eaten. My wife is a primary-school teacher: she tells me that when she asks her class where vegetables come from, most of the children say the supermarket. How difficult is it to plant a few spuds and sow a few seeds? You'll give your children a whole new perspective on food.

Roasted onion soup

Onions are easy to grow and easy to cook. They're the one vegetable we've always got to hand. Roasting the onions whole gives them a sweetness you cannot replicate in any other way. The recipe is inspired by the classic French soup, but it's a bit more interesting and a lot less effort.

INGREDIENTS

6 medium-sized white onions

2 garlic bulbs

2 sprigs of rosemary, plus a few extra leaves to serve

2 sprigs of fresh thyme

2 tbsp olive oil

1.2 litres (2 pints) vegetable stock

salt and black pepper

olive oil, to drizzle

For the croutons

8–10 slices baguette-type bread

100g (3½oz) soft goat's cheese

3 tbsp olive oil

Here's how

Preheat the oven to 160°C/325°F/Gas Mark 3.

Place the whole unpeeled onions on a roasting tray with the bulbs of garlic and herbs and drizzle with the olive oil. Cook them in the oven for 45 minutes – 1 hour, until soft and squidgy. Leave the oven on and turn it up to 180°C/350°F/Gas Mark 4.

Leave the onions and garlic to cool, then scoop out the insides of the onions and squeeze out the garlic into a pan. Keep any juices in the roasting tray to add to the finished soup (see below). Add the vegetable stock and blend until smooth. Season with salt and pepper to taste.

Make the croutons. Arrange the bread slices on a baking tray, crumble the goat's cheese on to the bread and drizzle with a little olive oil. Bake until golden and bubbling.

Pour the soup into a pan and heat gently. Season, drizzle with olive oil and the roasting juices from the onions and scatter with the reserved rosemary leaves. Serve with the croutons.

Courgette fritters

This recipe is great for vegetarians and meat eaters. If I can convert my carnivore dad to eating it, you can do the same. The fritters are really easy to make. I even cook them outside on a camp stove in the middle of the table when we have friends round for dinner in the garden.

INGREDIENTS

1kg (2lb) courgettes, grated

salt and black pepper

3 eggs

100g (3½oz) pecorino, grated

1 small onion, finely chopped

zest of 1 lemon

3 tbsp chopped flat-leaf parsley

1 tsp dried mint

4 tbsp olive oil

40g (1½oz) breadcrumbs

100g (3½oz) plain flour

To serve

olives

sliced red onions

salad leaves

cubed feta

pitta breads

Here's how

Season the grated courgettes with 2 tsp salt and leave for 30 minutes.

Whisk together the eggs and grated pecorino.

Preheat the oven to 160°C/325°F/Gas Mark 3.

Squeeze out as much liquid as you can from the courgettes and stir them into the eggs with the onion, lemon zest, parsley and mint, and stir to mix.

Add the breadcrumbs and flour, and combine together to form a soft mixture.

Pat the courgette mixture into small 'burger' shapes and arrange them on a lightly oiled baking tray. Drizzle the olive oil over the top of the courgette fritters and bake in the oven for 30 minutes.

Set out the olives, red onion, salad leaves and feta so that everyone can fill their own pittas.

Duck eggs with sprouting broccoli

For me ducks and sprouting broccoli mean summer is coming. I love it when I spot a container at the bottom of a farmer's lane full of tasty duck eggs for sale. When they are this fresh, less is more if you ask me. Just poach the eggs and serve with a simple plate of cooked broccoli.

INGREDIENTS

3 tbsp white wine vinegar

4 duck eggs

750g (1½lb) sprouting broccoli

smoked sea salt

Here's how

To poach 4 eggs at a time it's easier to use a wok than a saucepan, as it's larger and means there's more space around the eggs so they will cook better. Fill the wok with salted water, bring to the boil and add the vinegar. Carefully crack in the eggs and poach gently for 4–6 minutes. (Hen's eggs need about 3 minutes.)

Blanch the broccoli in boiling salted water for 2 minutes. Then divide between 4 plates, top each with a poached egg and sprinkle with a pinch of smoked sea salt.

Gnocchi with asparagus and Parmesan

This quick mid-week supper dish makes the most of British asparagus in season. Gnocchi make a nice change from pasta and, believe it or not, they cook even faster. Put them together with home-grown or freshly bought asparagus and a sprinkle of grated Parmesan.

INGREDIENTS

bunch of fresh asparagus

2 x 500g (1lb) packets shop-bought gnocchi

4 tbsp crème fraîche

100g (3½oz) Parmesan, grated

juice of ½ a lemon

handful of parsley, chopped

salt and black pepper

Here's how

Snap the ends off the asparagus wherever they break naturally – that's Mother Nature's way of telling us which bit of the stem is too tough to use.

Cook the gnocchi and the asparagus tops in boiling salted water until they start to bob up to the surface. As soon as they do, whip them off the heat and drain through a colander.

While they are cooking, heat a non-stick pan on a medium heat, then add the crème fraîche, grated Parmesan and lemon juice, and season with a little salt and pepper.

Stir in the gnocchi and asparagus, and check the seasoning before serving.

Pumpkin and chorizo soup

Pumpkins are easy plants, ideal for kids to help grow, and they make great soups. Roasted beforehand, the flesh takes on a fabulous sweetness. Then it becomes rich, smooth and velvety when you blend it – a lovely contrast to the cheeky smoky chorizo in this recipe. It's great served with walnut focaccia – the crunchy nuts in the bread are a good match with the soup.

INGREDIENTS

½ a pumpkin – approx 1kg (2lb)

1 white onion, chopped

1 tbsp olive oil

1 tsp ground cumin

4 garlic cloves, crushed

1.2 litres (2 pints) vegetable stock

150ml (¼ pint) double cream

salt and black pepper

100g (3½oz) good-quality chorizo, locally produced if you can get it

1 tbsp sherry vinegar

Here's how

Get out the biggest saucepan you have in the cupboard.

Peel and deseed the pumpkin, then chop it into chunks – about 2–3cm should be ok. Put them in the pan with the chopped onion, olive oil, cumin and garlic.

Set the pan on a medium heat – you want to get some colour on the pumpkin, so fry it for about 5–10 minutes.

Then add the vegetable stock and simmer for 40 minutes.

Blend the soup until smooth using a stick blender, then add the cream and taste for seasoning.

When you are ready to serve the soup, heat a small frying pan while you dice or slice the chorizo sausage. Cook it gently for a few minutes until the fat starts to melt, then stir in the sherry vinegar and remove from the heat.

Ladle the soup into bowls and top with some of the chorizo and the fat that has cooked out.

Spicy crunchy carrot salad

This is a great salad to serve with spicy food. Freshly pulled carrots are packed full of flavour as well as texture. The spicy, crispy croutons really give the salad some character – all finished off with a tangy dressing and loads of fresh and fragrant herbs.

INGREDIENTS

2 tbsp vegetable oil

2–3 tbsp curry powder

100g (3½oz) bread, torn into random chunks

2 tbsp white wine vinegar

3 tbsp olive oil

3 red onions

10 carrots

handful of sultanas

2 tbsp coriander seeds

2 tbsp poppy seeds

handful of coriander

salt and black pepper

Here's how

Preheat the oven to 160°C/325°F/Gas Mark 3.

Put the vegetable oil and curry powder in a mixing bowl with the torn-up bread and mix together to make sure all the bread is coated. Transfer the bread to a baking tray and bake until golden and crispy – 10–15 minutes.

Meanwhile in a salad bowl, mix together the vinegar and olive oil to make a dressing.

Chop the onions as finely as possible and add to the dressing. Wash and peel the carrots, then grate them straight into the bowl with the onion and dressing. Stir in the sultanas, coriander seeds and poppy seeds.

Remove the bread from the oven and leave to cool.

Roughly chop the fresh coriander and add to the salad.

Finally add the bread croutons, mix everything together, check the seasoning and serve.

Sweet 'n' sour sausages

When I think about British food and what we are truly good at producing, sausages have to be up there with the best. I live in Cumbria, home of the Cumberland sausage, and I'm spoilt for choice around here as we have so many great butchers. Sausages with these sweet and sour home-grown onions might sound simple but it's a perfect combination.

INGREDIENTS
6 red onions

salt and black pepper

3 tbsp olive oil

2–3 whole star anise

3 tbsp sherry vinegar

2 tsp sugar

8 Cumberland sausages

1 tsp chopped fresh thyme

Here's how

Preheat the oven to 180°C/350°F/Gas Mark 4.

Slice the onions as thinly as possible and put them in a casserole dish. Season with a little salt and pepper. Then add the olive oil, star anise, vinegar and sugar, cover and cook for 35 minutes.

Meanwhile, fry the sausages in a non-stick frying pan over a medium heat until brown – about 10 minutes.

Add the sausages to the casserole to finish cooking for the last 25 minutes. Sprinkle with the chopped thyme.

Fresh from the garden

Index

Index

Acknowledgements

I would like to thank my wife Emma, Poppy, the most amazing daughter I could wish for, and Thomas, who has completed my wonderful family. I would also like to thank once again Richard and Brenda Kealey, my in-laws, for their constant help, support and advice. And I would like to thank my mum and dad, without whose support I would have achieved nothing – I will always look up to you.

Thanks, too, to Dan Grimshaw, business partner and friend, for keeping me on schedule in the kitchen. And to all the kids who turned up to help me eat those yummy cakes and biscuits.

Peter Sidwell

Conversion tables

Approximate European/American conversion

	Metric	Imperial	USA
Breadcrumbs	50g	2oz	1 cup
Brown sugar	170g	6oz	1 cup
Butter	115g	4oz	1 cup
Butter/margarine/lard	225g	8oz	1 cup
Castor and granulated sugar	225g	8oz	1 cup
Currants	140g	5oz	1 cup
Flour	140g	5oz	1 cup
Golden syrup	350g	12oz	1 cup
Ground almonds	115g	4oz	1 cup
Hazelnuts, whole	150g	5oz	1 cup
Herbs, chopped	25g	1oz	1 cup
Oats	25g	1oz	1 cup
Sultanas/raisins	200g	7oz	1 cup

Liquid measurements

5ml	1 tsp
15ml	1 tbsp or ½ fl oz
25ml	1fl oz
50ml	2fl oz or ¼ cup
75ml	3fl oz
100ml	3½fl oz
125ml	4fl oz or ½ cup
150ml	5fl oz (¼ pint)
175ml	6fl oz
200ml	7fl oz
225ml	7½fl oz
250ml	8fl oz or 1 cup
275ml	9fl oz
300ml	½ pint or 1¼ cups
450ml	¾ pint
600ml	1pt (20fl oz)
1 litre	1¾ pints

Weights

15g	½oz	400g	13oz
25g	1oz	450g	14oz
50g	2oz	475g	15oz
75g	3oz	500g	1lb
100g	3½oz	625g	1¼lb
125g	4oz	750g	1½lb
150g	5oz	1kg	2lb
175g	6oz	1.25kg	2½lb
200g	7oz	1.5kg	3lb
225g	7½oz	1.75kg	3½lb
250g	8oz	2kg	4lb
275g	9oz		
300g	10oz		
325g	11oz		

Oven temperatures

°C	°F	Gas Mark	Oven
110	225	¼	
120	250	½	
140	275	1	Cool
150	300	2	
160	325	3	Moderate
180	350	4	
190	375	5	Moderately Hot
200	400	6	
220	425	7	Hot
230	450	8	
240	475	9	Very Hot

NB Cooking times for fan assisted ovens may be shorter. Please refer to manufacturers guidelines. All conversions are approximate.